KEEPING KIDS
CHRISTIAN

"This book is a must-read for parents, pastors, and congregations who need help with what it takes to intentionally partner with God's Spirit to create in children and their families a discipleship that lasts a lifetime. As challenging as it is practical and helpful, it gives clear and compelling ways to foster multigenerational relationships in congregations that nurture a maturity of faith for all God's children. *Keeping Kids Christian* offers a robust corrective to the viral dechurching of twenty-somethings walking out of the sanctuary and never returning."

Robbie Castleman, author of *Parenting in the Pew*
and *Story-Shaped Worship*

"Cameron Shaffer has written a generously diagnostic, biblically sound, and consistently edifying book that is as timely as it is helpful. We have needed an accessible, reliable guide to passing the faith down to the next generation(s) that is neither reactionary to problematic modern church practices nor blindly devoted to the better, older ways, and now we have it. Shaffer refreshingly—and rightly!—commends the old-new way of long-standing but recently forgotten Reformed conviction: the centrality of a healthy congregational, pastoral, and parental ecosystem for how God's garden grows. Pastors, teachers, other church leaders, moms, dads, grandparents, single Christians, older children—it is hard to imagine who doesn't need this book. I fully expect that those who read it will immediately want to share it, as I do, and that pastors and churches who heed even a little of the solid wisdom found here will be better for it."

Dr. Mark A. Garcia, president, Greystone Theological
Institute; associate professor of systematic theology,
Westminster Theological Seminary

"I wish I'd had this book when I started a new church plant some thirty years ago. We asked, 'What will we do with the children?' We got some of it right, but we would have gotten more of it right if Cameron Shaffer's book had been there to guide us. With depth and breadth of biblical and theological insight, Shaffer shows that lifelong discipleship matters and it takes a community to make a difference. This book is a wonderful starting point for anyone who is concerned about all generations of faith."

Rev. Jul Medenblik, president,
Calvin Theological Seminary

"Every pastor longs to help the children of the church remain faithful to the call of the gospel. In *Keeping Kids Christian*, Cameron Shaffer provides a historically aware, theologically rich, and practically wise guide for thoughtful shepherding and parenting of our covenant children. It is written for pastors, but parents would learn much from his counsel as well."

Dr. Scott Redd, lead pastor, Briarwood
Presbyterian Church

"Cameron Shaffer is an experienced pastor who, in this book, tackles one of the most pressing issues facing the evangelical church today—namely, how we can encourage our children to persevere in their faith as they enter their adult years. Whether or not one agrees with his theological description of covenant children, his advice to parents, pastors, and parishioners is of great value as we face this crucial challenge."

Sandy Willson, pastor emeritus, Second Presbyterian
Church, Memphis, Tennessee

KEEPING KIDS CHRISTIAN

RECOVERING A BIBLICAL VISION FOR LIFELONG DISCIPLESHIP

CAMERON S. SHAFFER

BakerBooks

a division of Baker Publishing Group
Grand Rapids, Michigan

© 2026 by Cameron Scott Shaffer

Published by Baker Books
a division of Baker Publishing Group
Grand Rapids, Michigan
BakerBooks.com

Printed in the United States of America

Library of Congress Cataloging-in-Publication Data
Names: Shaffer, Cameron Scott, 1989– author
Title: Keeping kids Christian : recovering a biblical vision for lifelong discipleship / Cameron Scott Shaffer.
Description: Grand Rapids, Michigan : Baker Books, a division of Baker Publishing Group, [2026] | Includes bibliographical references.
Identifiers: LCCN 2025020238 | ISBN 9781540905055 (paperback) | ISBN 9781540905376 (casebound) | ISBN 9781493452880 (ebook)
Subjects: LCSH: Christian education of children | Discipling (Christianity) | Parenting—Religious aspects—Christianity | Child rearing—Religious aspects—Christianity
Classification: LCC BV1475.3 .S539 2026 | DDC 268/.432—dc23/eng/20250903
LC record available at https://lccn.loc.gov/2025020238

Cover design by James Iacobelli

Some names and details have been changed to protect the privacy of the individuals involved.

Baker Publishing Group publications use paper produced from sustainable forestry practices and postconsumer waste whenever possible.

26 27 28 29 30 31 32   7 6 5 4 3 2 1

To Scott and Pam.
Thank you for raising me to know and love God.

Train up a child in the way he should go;
even when he is old he will not depart from it.

Proverbs 22:6

CONTENTS

FOREWORD

When Christians talk about parenting, it's easy to approach the conversation in the way an engineer might approach the task of building a complicated machine. Start by finding the right parts. Then assemble them together in a certain way. And at the end you can receive the desired outcome every time.

Applied to parenting decisions and Christianity, this means that we want to know what programs to put our kids in, what schools to send them to, what books to give them, what kind of youth pastor to look for at a church, what media or people to keep them away from.

We want parenting hacks, in other words. We want shortcuts to the desired outcomes that rely on relatively simple onetime actions: Take your kid to youth group at 7:00 p.m. every Wednesday during the school year, and this will produce a Christian kid at the end. That's parenting as engineering, and it has a certain appeal: It's relatively simple. It promises predictability. For many it will feel "safer."

But there's a problem with this approach: Children are not projects to be accomplished or problems to be solved. They are persons. As persons they long for a certain sort of relational presence in their lives and, indeed, merit such presence. What matters is not necessarily what they are taught but what is caught throughout their childhood and adolescence, what the atmosphere and timbre of their home and church teach them about the faith.

Children want to know they are loved, that they belong. They want to feel welcome in the world. To borrow from educators Bill and Maryellen St. Cyr, the question children are constantly asking us without words is this: "Is it good to be me, here with you?" We all want to be able to answer that question in the affirmative, of course.

But if we're going to offer that kind of belonging and connection to our children, it requires something more than engineered techniques and problem-solving. The trick is that answering that simple question—"Is it good to be me, here with you?"—isn't really the sort of thing we do once and then we're done, nor is it something we can outsource to other people to answer for us. Rather, it is a question we are answering constantly through the way we live.

If you're searching for another Christian-parenting-as-engineering-problem book, then this probably isn't what you're looking for. But if you're wanting something that probes more deeply, something that considers more basic questions about what it means to live in love and holiness before the face of God and among our neighbors—including the smallest and most vulnerable neighbors we have—then this book will offer you good counsel.

Cameron Shaffer's approach to Christian parenting is simply an account of Christian living applied to family life. As he presents it, parenting is not a discrete technical problem that must be solved. Rather, it is an element of Christian discipleship made possible by the same things that make every other aspect of the Christian life possible: God's active and purposeful love toward us and our response, in faith, to that love.

Parenting is an intense and demanding relationship, of course, and the roles of father and mother make certain demands on us that other titles do not. Even so, the task of Christian parents is simply to show their children Christ— and that is done not through bespoke youth group events or emotional manipulation but through the ordinary life of faith lived before the face of God and among God's people. Repeatedly Cam resists the attempt to "solve" our parenting woes through technical hacks and calls us back instead to the ordinary means of grace. His confidence in those means is inspiring and encouraging and a great reminder to us that the same means Christ used to call us to himself are the ones he will use to do that for our children.

For too long we American Protestants have been inordinately fond of the "one simple trick," the life hack, the technique. Too often we have done as the Ephesian church did and forgotten our first love. If we are to return to health, then we must return to that love.

What makes this book so helpful and worthy of your attention is that in it you'll find a pastor reflecting on how a person given to that love would go about loving and caring for children. Too often we have put the cart before the horse in our thinking about parenting, as Cameron rightly notes. This is a book in which first things are allowed to be first—and then we are allowed to answer the questions we have about that most practical and challenging thing, caring for our children.

Jake Meador, editor in chief of *Mere Orthodoxy*

INTRODUCTION

The single greatest religious shift in American history is underway, driven by children of the church walking away from the Christian faith.

Like many pastors, I have seen this sociological reality play out both in my communities and in the faces of friends and family who have left the faith. Many parents and grandparents in my church are in anguish over children they raised to love Jesus becoming indifferent or hostile to him. And parents in my congregation with young children are watching nervously as their peers reject the faith in droves and their own children enter a world where Christian belief and practice are no longer not even assumed but actively treated as foreign.[1] As both a pastor and a parent of young children, I share the same concern as my friends and congregants—I want my kids to keep their faith in Christ into and through adulthood. This is not just a professional interest; it's deeply personal.

In the span of twenty-five years, the percentage of Americans identifying as Christian dropped from roughly 85 percent in 1990 to 65 percent in 2015.[2] For the first time in

American history, less than 50 percent of the nation identifies as Protestant.[3] By 2018, the "Nones"—people without a self-identified religious affiliation—were as large a group as Roman Catholics and evangelical Protestants, and by 2024 they were the single largest religious group in the country.[4] This group represented only about 10 percent in 1990, yet it is the single largest religious demographic for Millennials and Gen Z and is on track to outnumber Protestants of all traditions combined by 2030.[5]

Ryan P. Burge in *The Nones* demonstrates that the rise of the religiously unaffiliated is driven by children of religious parents increasingly not adopting their family's faith. In *The Great Dechurching*, Burge, Jim Davis, and Michael Graham examine how the rise of the Nones was fueled by the disaffiliation of the religious "in name only" crowd and by those who grew up actively engaged in church.[6]

At the same time as this dechurching, a cottage industry of "deconversion" publications has developed: books and podcasts devoted to the individualized experience of former Christians, across the full range of denominational traditions, who share their story of growing up Christian and then repudiating the faith.[7] While anecdotal by nature, the narrative details easily map onto the sociological landscape charted by Burge, Davis, and Graham.

In response to this shift toward dechurching and deconversion, the church has undertaken a renewed effort to regain lost ground and lost people. Apologists have sprung into action in an attempt to address deconversion stories, insulate adults tempted in that direction, and win back those who have rejected Christianity.

This shift in religious affiliation—and the departure of so many from the Christian faith—is one of the most important ministerial realities facing pastors and churches. The efforts to share the gospel and lead prodigal sheep back home are noble and important. So yes, evangelism must guide the de-churched home and shepherd the lost into Christ's kingdom, but simply growing the numbers in a church that is leaking like a sieve ignores the deeper problems that produced this situation. The church's kids are leaving it behind, and reckoning with the reason the church has lost so many from its fold and adjusting its practices to retain its children are both absolutely crucial.[8] The church must act now.

In 2021 sociologists Amy Adamczyk and Christian Smith published *Handing Down the Faith*, which built on well-known sociological research about childhood faith retention.[9] Sociologists have known for decades that parental influence overwhelmingly determines whether people hold on to their childhood faith as they grow.

Most churches' resource allocation and ministry strategies are dominated by Sunday school, confirmation, vacation Bible school (VBS), kids' ministry coordinators, youth groups, youth pastors, short-term mission trips and service projects, and the like. The apparent venerability of these programmatic strategies provides a sense of their indispensable contribution to faith retention, but none of them reflect the truth that parents are far and away the most crucial factor for passing along a lasting faith to children. A common refrain pastors hear from their children and youth ministry leaders is that they wish parents understood that the ministry needs parental engagement if it's going to be helpful for the kids. This is true, but backward: Children's and youth ministry are supplementary, at best, to what parents are doing at home. In other words, the *vast* energy that churches spend trying to get parents invested in kids' programming so it's effective is misallocated. Investing in the parents directly is far more effective.

Sociologists have known this since the 1970s, yet the American church somehow continues to overlook it. Adamczyk and Smith both reaffirmed this data and analyzed the parenting styles and practices that were most effective across religious traditions in handing the faith from one generation to the next. These styles and practices are authoritative parenting with faith as a lifestyle (by a wide margin the most important), with channels to express that lifestyle, particularly incorporation into the liturgical and communal practices of the religion. Alarmingly, they also noted how things like Sunday school, confirmation, and youth group can actually be counterproductive to faith retention.

My goal in this book is to apply observations like Adamczyk and Smith's as well as Burge's to the church's programmatic strategy. In light of what we know about how faith is passed down and retained across generations, how should the church allocate its resources and organize its ministry programs?

In the arena of children and family ministry, there is a long debate and a large publishing industry surrounding ministry best practices, especially when it comes to youth ministry. The nature of the debate is really about where a church's kids' ministry should fall along a spectrum, with fun, welcoming, adolescent vibes on one end and rigorous biblical and theological study on the other. Rather than enter that debate, I want to challenge its whole premise.

The question is not whether to have a youth group that is either silly or studious; it is how to justify having a youth group at all if the goal is to help kids retain their faith. This is not tinkering with or adjusting the details of a framework for discipleship; it is the case for an entirely different approach.[10] The prioritization of this framework fueled the great dechurching, and while there may be a place for these programs in a church's ministry, they should be downgraded in importance and treated as risky for faith retention.

I am a pastor, not a sociologist or psychologist. The following chapters utilize sociological and psychological data, but I'm interested in the church's practice. I'm a Protestant, Reformed, Presbyterian, and evangelical minister, which means I unashamedly hold to the Scriptures as the only rule for faith and practice, and I believe the church is conscience-bound only by what God has revealed in his Word. My vocation is pastoral ministry, so while my writing is informed by sociological insights, I will be writing on ministry practices. And since God's Word is the church's final authority, one of my goals will be to show the overlap between what sociologists have noted and what Scripture reveals. I unapologetically hold to Reformed theological convictions, but the following arguments for practices in the church apply to any denominational context.

This book's aim is to help fellow pastors and ministry leaders think through how the church can work in their context to ensure that their kids stay Christian, though it is written in such a way that interested laypeople can learn by "listening in." This is not a parenting book. While parenting is the most important aspect of kids staying Christian, the focus here is on how the church can go about its work of ministering to children. Like with children and youth programming, the insights for ministry to parents will also splash over to provide some understanding into how to better parent. Similarly, the practice of family discipleship and the crucial role of fathers in particular for faith development are not the focus of this book, though information related to these topics will surface. This is a *how* book, not a how-to book, even if it is replete with concrete examples. The aim is to provide a model for lifelong discipleship, not specific programmatic guidance.

The book's focus is on how the church in its ministry practices can retain its children and proactively head off the great dechurching. The following chapters will discuss the different sociological observations in conversation with theological analysis, with recommendations on the practical application. To that end, this book lays out the biblical foundations for how childhood conversion happens to help churches minister to families and kids (chapter 1). The crucial role parents play in faith retention will be explored, with consideration to both sociological research and scriptural wisdom (chapter 2). Pastors must know the principles of parental influence as well as teach and model them in warm, authoritative ways in order to equip parents to sincerely model that same warmth and authority in the daily rhythms of faith (chapter 3). Rather than isolating children in age-segregated programming, churches must intentionally incorporate them into their gathered worship and their broader life (chapter 4), ensuring they are known and discipled as full members of the family of Christ (chapter 5).

Finally, this book will emphasize the importance of fostering a faith ecosystem rather than relying on programs (chapter 6). As children grow into adulthood, the influence of their parents continues, but churches also have a role in supporting them through key life transitions (chapter 7). By taking this approach—one that integrates theology, sociological insights, parenting, pastoral leadership, and church community, resting upon the good grace of God for the salvation of our children—we can recover a biblical vision for lifelong discipleship.

Chapter 1

BORN INTO GOD'S FAMILY
Discipling Children as Believers

On Easter morning in 1996, I was sitting in the back pew of the church alongside my family. I was a young boy and had grown up in a Christian home where the Bible was faithfully taught. The biblical story of Jesus Christ was part of the fabric of my life and was just as true for me as the sky was blue, the grass was green, and any other obvious facets of kid life. But that morning as I listened to my pastor, I realized that if the biblical story was real, then I needed to respond to it in some way. I bowed my head and said a prayer asking Jesus to save me from my sins. That was clearly a moment of faith, but it is also true that I cannot recall a single prior moment when I didn't believe the gospel.

In order to understand how our kids remain Christian, we need to first grasp how they become Christians. The church is often caught between two competing, unhelpful impulses on childhood salvation. The first is that since salvation is a work of God by his grace alone, the influence of the church and family on a child's salvation is only incidental or providential, not something to be intentionally worked toward. The other is that a child's Christian identity can be assumed or planned through their participation in a family or church, as if God's direct and miraculous involvement in their heart were an inconsequential afterthought rather than an absolute necessity that is beyond our power to compel.

Proverbs 22:6 says, "Train up a child in the way he should go; even when he is old he will not depart from it." On the one hand, we need to avoid any mechanistic, naturalistic impulses concerning our children's faith and depend upon God's grace for their salvation and perseverance therein. On the other hand, we need to acknowledge that God has established regular, ordinary means of producing that faith and work to foreground these in our churches, our families, and the lives of our children.

When either mechanistic or fatalistic approaches dominate discipleship of kids, faith retention weakens, and many children do not continue in Christianity or the church into adulthood. Scripture teaches that salvation is the work of the Holy Spirit, not something we can manufacture, and pastors must begin there to properly orient the church's efforts for lifelong discipleship. The Bible presents faith as a covenant reality—children are already part of the church community and should be discipled as such, rather than being treated as outsiders who must become Christians later even as the church seeks their sincere profession of faith. This view shapes the kinds of tools and approaches the church uses to guide children toward lasting faith and establishes a biblical foundation for the approaches to be discussed throughout the rest of the book.

How Does God Save? His Holy Spirit

How does a child become a Christian? That question has many layers to it. It could be rephrased as "How is a child saved?," which in turn can be further distilled (or expanded!) to "How does a child come to possess saving faith in Jesus Christ, in which their spiritually dead heart is regenerated with his life as they are united to him and justified?" How does someone go from being spiritually dead to being born again in Christ?

John's Gospel takes up this question right from its prologue. In John 1:12–13, the apostle affirms that anyone who receives Jesus and believes in his name becomes a child of God. He draws a distinction between groups of people: those who reject Jesus and those who receive him. The implication is that everyone starts in a position of nonacceptance and that receiving Jesus is a necessary condition of becoming a child of God. In other words, we don't *start* as children of God but *become* children of God through Christ. "Become children of God" is both John's shorthand describing the act of salvation and the highest blessing of salvation: fellowship with God our Father as his children.

Becoming children of God necessitates a rebirth as his children. And this birth occurs "not of blood nor of the will of the flesh nor of the will of man, but of God" (v. 13). What causes someone to receive Christ and become a child of God? John rules out three possibilities. First, it is not genetic or biological. People are not saved on the basis of their physical makeup or lineage. Second, it is not something conjured up or willed by the person needing to be saved. There's nothing inherent in us that empowers us to will our own salvation, the movement from death to life. Third, it's not the will of man, literally "husband" in Greek. Salvation is not something we can marry into. Or, to put a fine point on it, salvation is not a social benefit. Joining the right group, whether a family, church, neighborhood, or nation, does not unite someone by faith to Jesus.

Reception of Christ and becoming a child of God happens by the act of God himself. On this level, there is nothing anyone can do to save another person, including our beloved children. We wait with humility and patience upon the sovereign will and mercy of God.

John 3 expands on this idea in the famous nighttime encounter between Nicodemus and Jesus. Nicodemus asserts that he knows Jesus is from God, but Jesus quickly corrects him: "Unless one is born again he cannot see the kingdom of God" (v. 3). Nicodemus claims to know Jesus, but Christ is telling him that in actuality he doesn't. Nicodemus needs a transformation, to be born again, in order to truly see Jesus for who he is. The Greek phrase *anothen*, typically translated "born again," has a double meaning and can also be understood as "born from above." Nicodemus doesn't take it that way and responds, perhaps sarcastically or even overliterally, "How can someone be born again and reenter his mother's womb?" (see v. 4).

Nicodemus is no dummy. The real issue here is that he hasn't considered that he is lacking something to know and see Christ. Jesus pushes back yet again and more clearly explains that new life has to come from above. He goes on to explain in verses 13–14 that since he is the Christ who descended from heaven, he is the one who is able to provide this renewed life from above. To be born again is to have the life of heaven, the life of Christ, dispensed by Jesus in his ministry.

People need to be renewed in the life of Christ, via the Spirit of Christ (vv. 5–6), in order to enter the kingdom of

God. Like begets like, and any new life apart from this reality is just the same old life in the flesh. Life in the Spirit of God is necessary to see and enter the kingdom of God.

Jesus heads off any misconception that being born again or from above can happen in any way other than through the divine intervention of the Holy Spirit. He explains that the born-again or born-above life is given from the Spirit, and the Spirit is like the wind. (Here Jesus uses another word with a double meaning, *pneuma*. "Spirit," "wind," and "breath" in Greek all use the same word.) The Spirit acts and goes where he wills. We can't see or control or channel the wind, and in the same way, the Holy Spirit does as he pleases in providing people renewed life.

In other words, to become a child of God, saved by being united to Jesus, people need to be born of God, which occurs only through the sovereign prerogative of the Holy Spirit. We are saved by Christ giving us his Holy Spirit, who is the provision of Christ's life to us.

Any ministry practice for children or approach to discipleship of them must absolutely start here. We cannot control or channel the Spirit but must instead act in humble patience, trusting in God's grace to provide salvation. Our children are born again as children of God, not by their being special, not by our efforts to disciple them, not by their belonging to the right church or youth group, but from above as the Holy Spirit acts according to the counsel of his wise and holy will.

Conversion Comes by Faith in Christ

To convert to Christianity means, at this first layer, to be united to Jesus. Throughout the New Testament, particularly the letters of Paul, this language of being united to

Jesus, "in Christ," is a dominant way of describing the nature of the Christian's relationship to Jesus. We are "in" him, and he is in us. We are tied together—he is the vine, we are the branches, and we abide in him, meaning that he is the source and flow of our life. When we speak of becoming a Christian and converting, this is what we must first mean: participating in the life of Christ because we have been united to him.

This is not something we can create on our own but is the mystical work of the Holy Spirit. "In Christ" is the real and true being and status of the Christian. No one is conceived being united to Christ, but we are transferred from spiritual alienation to union with Christ by the work of God. This happens by faith, which is the gift of God to sinners. John 1 says that to become a child of God, one needs to receive Christ. That means welcoming and embracing him. In John 3 Jesus clarifies that becoming a child of God—rebirth from above by the Spirit's work—comes through looking to the Son. Jesus compares himself to the bronze serpent Moses raised in Numbers 21. At that time, God was punishing his disobedient people by sending venomous snakes among them. Moses erected a bronze staff, which looked like a snake, on a hill. Anyone who had been bitten by a snake would be healed and spared if they looked at the staff.

There was nothing magical about the staff, nor was God setting up weird conditions for salvation. The point of that exercise was to remind us that the wages of sin is death, but the free gift of God is eternal life. The people of Israel, like us, did nothing to earn that salvation. Those poisoned by the snakes were invited to trust God for salvation; all they had to do was look at the staff. All they had to do was trust that God would save. And all we do is rest upon and trust the promise of God for salvation. Faith is receiving and resting upon what God has promised.

Jesus tells Nicodemus that true salvation—not from poison but from sin, death, and judgment—comes in the same way. Just look; just trust. In our case, we look not to a raised serpent but to Jesus raised on a cross for our salvation. Simply having faith in Jesus, receiving and resting upon him as he is offered in the gospel, is the instrument by which the Holy Spirit grants rebirth from above to people.

Conversion happens by faith—true belief and trust in Christ. Our churches and ministries tend to be really good about one part of faith: "You've got to believe, and it has to be your own and not someone else's faith! Salvation is by faith, so you have to believe for yourself." This is absolutely true but is only one-half of reality, and left by itself it can lead to warped practices and outcomes.

The danger pastors sometimes fall into is functioning as if we can persuade people into faith. Now, Christianity is reasonable and rational, and we should strive for persuasiveness and rationality in showcasing our faith, especially to our children. However, many children's and youth programs, especially youth retreats and mission trips, have an element of manipulation to them, where we plan to say just the right things in just the right way at just the right time in order to compel people into faith. Confirmation classes can be especially dangerous in this regard. Godly parents who really hope their kids come to faith, children who desperately want to please their parents and fit in with their friends, pastors and teachers who want their faithful labors to bear obvious fruit—these create the perfect storm for pressured, false confession of faith. We tell kids what we believe, what they should believe, and what words to say or projects to do, and then treat them at the end of that time as if they have sincere faith because they went through a class.

But faith cannot be manufactured, either by us laboring for our children or by our children themselves. Being reborn as a child of God does not happen by the flesh, by the will, or by our social connections. It happens from God. The Holy Spirit works faith in us; faith itself is a gift from God, whereby we are enabled to believe as our wills and minds are renewed in the likeness of Christ. The gospel and salvation are the gracious work of God alone, from start to end and in the middle. Knowing God—having faith—comes from God himself in our being reborn from above.

Our ministries need to always foreground the gracious, undeserved, and unmerited work of God, including his work in drawing us to himself by faith. The need for genuine, saving faith should never be presumed. Without that faith our children are not united to Jesus; only through it are our kids "in Christ" alongside us. Devoted labor, ministry, and parenting should occur for the sake of planting and nurturing faith, but any confidence in our kids staying Christian (i.e., staying united to Jesus) needs to start here. Otherwise we rest upon sociological or social status and then see generations walk away from Christianity. Otherwise we rest upon the efficacy of our ministerial programs and youth groups, then spin our wheels as we try to reinvent something that cannot provide eternal life in the first place. Otherwise we feel betrayed by God when we do everything "right" and then faith doesn't stick with our kids.

Salvation in Christ and the faith by which he is received come from the Holy Spirit, and we cannot channel him into the hearts of our youngsters. Our children staying Christian is then God's work and responsibility. He calls and holds his people, and he who unites his children to Christ alone can maintain their union with him.

Because faith comes from God, we can trust and follow the ordinary means he has established for providing it.

Conversion Comes by God's Covenant

I'm an American because I was born an American. I was not merely born in US territory but am descended from generations of Americans, going back to before the Revolution and all the way to the Dutch colonization of New Amsterdam (Manhattan). My fathers and mothers are buried in American soil all across the continent, and I am deeply formed by American culture, institutions, history, and practices. People from countries across the globe can speak of their national identities in similar ways. Yet one popular way of describing America as unique among nations focuses on its ideological foundation: a country established to secure self-evident truths about human rights and happiness. America is not only a people, place, and history but also a commitment to ideals.

I was an American by birth long before I could understand these ideals, much less articulate, agree with, and defend them. I was taught our story; instructed in our civics; shown the beauty of our nation and ideals (Memorial Day parades and Fourth of July fireworks do wonders to instill affection in children for a country); and formed in the values of liberty, equality, and democracy as I grew. America was my heritage and inheritance by birthright long before I ever grasped the meaning and responsibilities of that gift. My parents and grandparents never said things like, "We don't want to pass our citizenship on to him because we want him to decide to be an American on his own as an adult." They treated me as an American who needed to be trained in responsible citizenship.

God operates in the same way with his people. The clearest picture of this is with the Old Testament people of God, the nation of Israel. God called Abram from the land of Ur and made a covenant with him. A covenant is a kind of pledge or agreement, but with greater weight. Theologians and scholars of the ancient Near Eastern world have proposed multiple definitions for "covenant," including "a bond in blood sovereignly administered"[1] and "a stipulated commitment under divine sanctions."[2] But the easiest one to remember and teach to children is "A relationship that God establishes with us and guarantees by his word."[3] A covenant is the kind of relationship that God creates and sets the terms for, and he is the one who guarantees its terms. His word is his bond and the collateral for the fulfillment of the relationship.

The specific covenant made with Abram was that he would be made a great nation through many descendants, that he would be granted the land of Canaan as a home for his people, and that God would bless him and the world through his descendants (Gen. 12:1–3; 15:4–5). This pledge was always about salvation in Christ, not merely having kids, grandkids, and a plot of land to build a home. Abram trusted God's promise, "I will be a God to you and your children," and it was counted to him as righteousness.

God's covenant with Abram was developed and fleshed out over time, but a key milestone was delivering his descendants, numbering hundreds of thousands, from slavery in Egypt. Abram's descendants were known as the Hebrew people, the nation of Israel. God confirmed with them through Moses that they were heirs of the covenant promises to Abram, and as the nation and community that inherited that promise, they received another covenant that detailed the rules, expectations, and blessings of being the people of God. To be born to an Israelite was to be born an inheritor of the promises of God. "I will be a God to you and your children."

Covenants in the ancient world came with signs and seals that represented their substance. In God's covenant with David, for instance (2 Sam. 7:1–16; Jer. 33:20–21), David's throne was God's sign and seal of his promise. The covenant with Abram had the sign and seal of circumcision. Circumcision had the dual purpose of assuring the people of God's promise and reminding them that they were parties to the covenant, which brings with it both the promises of God and the expectations of belonging to him. Circumcision was so closely identified with the covenant that God actually calls it the covenant itself (Gen. 17:9–13), and it being marked on the body of male Israelites served as an indelible reminder of who they were, by virtue of the promise of God.

To be born an Israelite was to be born a child of the covenant. To be a descendant of Abraham, Isaac, and Jacob, a member of the nation with its rules and customs defined by the covenant made under Moses, was to be an Israelite. And an Israelite individually was a child of the covenant: a child of the promise of God for salvation.

In this sense, under the terms of the covenant relationship that God established, a child of God is someone who belongs to the covenant community of God. Sometimes modern Christians denigrate the Old Testament community of God as "just" a political or cultural entity. It's as if there were two Old Testament peoples of God: first, the Israelites who received the covenants and Mosaic law, defined by rules, regulations, and cultures, but for whom being a child of God was not actually spiritual and salvific; and second, the Israelites who had faith in God and incidentally were required to be part of the first community as an act of obedience.

It's true that as the history of redemption progresses, the community of God finds its fuller expression in the New Testament church under Christ's rule. But the communities formed by God's covenants are always aimed at the same thing: his glory in our enjoyment of him through salvation in Jesus Christ. This was just as true of the Old Testament covenant community of national Israel as it is of the New Testament covenant community of the Christian church. People of the covenant are not just discrete individuals, converted and united to Jesus by faith and then joined together for worship and discipleship. Covenant communities are families God has established for the sake of passing down and enculturating the faith in its members.

To be born an Israelite was to be born, in this sense, into the family of God, with his promise of salvation as their birthright and inheritance. This is how the New Testament talks about the Old Testament Jewish people (see Rom. 9:1–5). A Jewish baby born into the nation of Israel was a child of God by covenant; they were in the family of God by virtue of the relationship that God established and guaranteed by his word. A child, in this sense, becomes a follower of God by covenant.

How does this not contradict salvation by faith alone? Because the covenant family of God, with all its rules, regulations, customs, and expectations, was intended to cultivate faith in God. Even circumcision was a call to regeneration (Deut. 10:16; 30:6). The things that marked the boundaries of the covenant community were also calls to faith.

Circumcision as a sign of the covenant was an indelible mark in the flesh that renewed life—not only in the body but in the heart and soul—and was necessary for salvation, which God alone could truly provide.

The cairn stones were set up to remind the children of the Old Testament of God's miraculous salvation (Exod. 13:3–6; 24:4; Deut. 27:1–8; Josh. 4:9). The signs of the covenant were more than markers of the earthly family of God; they were the earthly means of calling children of Israel to faith in God, whereby they were united to Jesus. As God said to Abram, "I will establish my covenant between me and you and your offspring after you throughout their generations for an everlasting covenant, to be God to you and to your offspring after you" (Gen. 17:7).

This covenant principle continues from the Old to the New Testament; now circumcision and the Passover lamb have been fulfilled in the death of Jesus, who in the new covenant has given his church the signs and seals of baptism and the Lord's Supper to exhibit the relationship that he has established with the church and guarantees by his word. The promise of God remains for those who trust in God by faith in Christ. The covenant community is still the family of God aimed at enculturating faith in Christ: "For the promise is for you and for your children . . . , everyone whom the Lord our God calls to himself" (Acts 2:39).

Conversion has a community and a corporate identity. Israelites were Israelites by virtue of God's promise. Salvation was never by blood or birth but by the promise of God (the covenant) received by faith. They could be described as Israelites by birth and blood because they were heirs of the promise, but they were Israelites truly by faith, insofar as their hearts were circumcised by God through trust in his promises.

The same is true for children of the church. It is faith in the person and work of Jesus that saves, but we can also describe our children as being Christian insofar as they are part of the community that has received the promises of God: the church. The covenant community of God works in the same way. Conversion, then, is about receiving the promises of God through the normal things of the world, which are gifts that God uses to work faith for the sake of union with Christ. This connection between covenant community and faith is what Paul reminds Timothy of regarding his upbringing—that his sincere faith was passed down to him by his grandmother Lois and mother Eunice (2 Tim. 1:5; 3:14–15).

Every Christian belongs to the community formed by God's covenant promises: the church of Christ. To be abundantly clear, being born to Christian parents does not unite a child to Jesus by faith. But just as the children of Israelites were themselves Israelites, children born to Christian parents who are part of the church receive the blessings of the church as their heritage and inheritance. In this sense, to convert to Christianity is to belong to the community forged by God's covenant—to join the church by becoming a participant in God's covenant of grace.

The church, its ministry, and its community are the natural, God-ordained means for nurturing faith in the children of Christians. The church and its ministries are the ordinary means by which grace is distributed to and received by the children of God. Kids become Christians through participation in the life of the church. They stay Christian through their rootedness in the church's faith and practice, and the vehicle that normally brings them into the life of the church is their family—namely, their parents.

The Church Needs to Treat Its Kids as Christians

There are several implications that flow from the covenant nature of God's people, and one of them is that the church should presume the children of Christian parents are themselves Christians. The church is not to act as missionaries to its children, as if they were non-Christians living outside the kingdom of God, but should disciple them as those to whom the kingdom of God belongs. Conversion and union with Christ occur by faith, but that does not preclude the church from describing its children as being Christian before they have expressed that faith.

The first reason for this freedom is due to the covenant, community nature of the church. The second is that the church should presume the presence of saving faith in its children even prior to their articulation of that faith. Saving faith is not rational assent to the precepts of Christian dogma, though it does necessitate that as a consequence. Saving faith is a regenerated heart that trusts God. Like how children implicitly trust, rest upon, and cry out for their earthly parents before they can articulate the nature of their relationship, children can trust in their heavenly Father before being able to express the reasonable nature of their faith.

A good biblical example of this is John the Baptist in the womb of his mother, Elizabeth. In Luke 1:41–44 when the pregnant Elizabeth hears Mary's greeting, the preborn John recognizes the preborn Jesus across the distance of the two wombs. John leaps and kicks for joy; he is acting in a regenerated manner even before being born. The Holy Spirit descended upon John in the womb and regenerated him, granting him faith and union with Jesus even before he was born, much less able to speak words of faith. John was not saved differently than any other person; he was saved by the indwelling of the Holy Spirit, who provides faith. The difference is the clear example of the timing and the unusual circumstances in which God provided for the conception and ministry of John.

When Jesus welcomed children to join him (Matt. 19:13–14; Mark 10:13–16), he welcomed even infants (Luke 18:15–17) and announced that the kingdom of God belonged to those like them. He was not saying that adults with a child-like faith were part of the kingdom while the infants themselves were out. He was saying instead that the kingdom of God, which no one can see or enter without rebirth from above, belonged even to these very young children. Infants before they can speak, and toddlers before they can recite the Apostles' Creed with understanding, have the faith from the Holy Spirit that brings one into the kingdom.

Confirmation (or communicant) classes are good examples of this principle in action. These classes, if done well, are designed not to draw faith out of a child or to create faith in them. Rather, they exist to confirm to the child, their family, and the church the existence of that presumed faith, by equipping the child to sincerely articulate what it is they believe. They are built to confirm or exhibit faith, where presumed faith transforms into professed faith. The church approaches its children as baby Christians who need to grow in their communion with Jesus.

By nature, kids are children of wrath because they are sinners who are in bondage to the power of Satan and in need of a Savior (Eph. 2:1–4). But by covenant, kids of Christian parents, kids of the church, are holy. To be holy is to be devoted to God, set aside and dedicated to him on his terms. By virtue of belonging to Christian parents—parents who themselves belong to the one holy church—children of believers are holy.

This is why Paul can talk about the children of one believing parent and one nonbelieving parent as holy (1 Cor. 7:14–15). They are already heirs of the covenant promises of God and are recipients of the normal, temporal benefits of belonging to the covenant community. As children of the covenant, we presume that our kids have been welcomed by Jesus into his kingdom, and we disciple them accordingly. In the Old Testament, the Israelites were commanded to teach their children the Shema: "Hear, O Israel: the LORD our God, the LORD is one" (Deut. 6:4). Children, even infants, received this creedal statement and were expected to be taught it and recite it with honesty. Their parents were not coercing the children to recite what wasn't true of them. By covenant, the Lord was indeed the God of the kids of Israel, and the parents, with eagerness to have their children discipled, were to teach them to heartily recite those words.

In the same way, Christian parents and the church can teach their children to pray, "Our Father, who art in heaven" long before the kids can articulate their own personal faith. God is the Father of those who have been united by faith to God the Son, yet parents can teach their children to pray to their heavenly Father even from the youngest age, when vocabularies are first developing, long before a child is capable of vocalizing their personal beliefs. Why? Because they are children of the covenant who belong to the church through the normal gift of a family and can be honestly described as Christians who are being discipled, not non-Christians who need to be evangelized. Their status in the church is members—nonprofessing members, but members of God's people through his covenant all the same.

The Ordinary Means of Grace: The Church's Toolbelt

Family and the church itself are the normal and natural gifts that God has given his people to ensure that faith in Christ is passed down. The rest of this book concerns the posture, culture, and hope for the regular rhythms of family and church life to strive for so our children stay Christian. Salvation and union with Christ are not mechanistic but are works of God's sovereign grace exercised within the context of these normal communities. And God uses tools (means) to normally and ordinarily apply the benefits of Christ's redemptive work (grace) to his people. These are the Word of God, prayer, and the sacraments. The clearest biblical statement to this effect is found in Romans 10:17: "Faith comes from hearing, and hearing through the word of Christ."

If we want our kids to be united to Jesus, to grow in communion with him, and to profess sincere faith in him, then our churches and homes need to be characterized by devotion to the ordinary means of grace. These means are made effective for salvation not by the efforts and skills of those administering them or the quality of the recipients but by the appointment of Christ and the operation of the Holy Spirit. Christ established these practices, and the Holy Spirit uses them to bring the gospel to bear on the hearts of those who receive them, so that faith may be worked in their souls and they turn to Christ. If a church wants its kids to be Christians by faith and to remain in the grace of God, then whatever programs and culture it may have must be characterized by these practices and ordinances.

First, the Word of God must shape the church's programs and culture, for it is through Scripture that we come to know God. Through the preaching of the Word, the Spirit works to create and strengthen faith in its hearers. As we immerse our minds and wills in Scripture, we are transformed—no longer conformed to a sinful world but renewed by God's truth. Saturating our churches and children in the Word and cultivating a sincere love for it are essential for them to know God. He uses his Word to train, educate, and form his people, producing and bolstering faith. By listening to Scripture, children learn to recognize the voice of their Father—just as the sheep learn to know the voice of Jesus (John 10:16, 27). The Word of God contains his covenant promises, written and proclaimed, given to his people so they may know the substance of that promise: Christ crucified and received by faith.

Because the divine gift of faith is presumed present by covenant, children are to receive the Word of God both as covenant members and as those who need to grow in faith. The Word is to be preached so as to draw people to faith, salvation, and conversion. Children, no more or less than adults, need the nurturing of the Word.

The second ordinary means of grace is prayer. Prayer is asking God for things that are agreeable to his will and character, and that certainly includes praying for the salvation and spiritual formation of our children. Prayer is the acknowledgment that the normal, visible powers of cause and effect are not all there is to the universe, that there is a God, that he is powerful, and that he can do all that he pleases. In other words, prayer is us as his children turning to this God for help for *our* children. Teaching our children to pray and praying for our children are some of the highest blessings that come with being part of God's covenant community.

This is the key: The Word of God is his covenant address to his people, wherein his gospel promise is announced and we're reminded of the grace of Jesus. Prayer is our covenant response to God, wherein we who are parties to the gospel cry out in the name of Jesus and the power of the Spirit to our heavenly Father. Prayer is the practice of our personal relationship to God. We as his children come to our loving Father. Teaching our children to pray is teaching them to know God—to hear his voice in his Word and to speak to him as one who hears and cares for us. Prayer is an act of faith, where through the mediation of Christ and the power of the Holy Spirit, God's children lift their hearts, souls, and minds to their Father and grow in communion with him. Prayer knits our hearts more deeply to God. Teaching our children to pray is not simply teaching them a model and posture but walking with them down the most basic path of faith: We may not see him, but there is a God, he hears you, and he cares for you, because he is our heavenly Father.

The sacraments of baptism and the Lord's Supper are together the third ordinary means of grace. Sacraments are signs and seals of God's covenant that represent and communicate to us the substance of the gospel promise of Jesus. They affirm the covenant promise of God, and since they are divinely established, they come with divine authority and power.

Baptism marks admission into God's covenant family, the church. It represents the promise of God that as surely as one is washed in water, if they turn to God through faith in Jesus Christ, their soul is cleansed of sin. The Word preached is the covenant announced, prayer is speaking to God as his covenant children, and the sacraments are the covenant Word made visible in water, bread, and wine.

Now, baptism is not only the marker of admission but also a means by which the Holy Spirit accomplishes what it represents. This is the exact same as the preaching of the Word: It is not sound waves in the air from a pastor's mouth or the reverberation in a person's ear that creates faith. God the Spirit uses the sounds and words and meanings as the avenue by which he creates and builds faith. It does not happen automatically whenever someone hears Scripture taught, but only at the Spirit's discretion is the Word used to bring people to faith. Baptism is the same. It is not water or the motions of the pastor in washing a child that regenerates; that only happens by faith as the Holy Spirit works. But like with the spoken Word, the Spirit uses the waters of baptism as the covenant promises of God made visible (rather than audible in the Word) to create and build up the faith of our children.[4] Baptism is a Christ-established means by which the union of children with Christ is confirmed and our communion with him strengthened, and it serves as a lifelong blessing for those who receive it since it is a gift of Jesus.

The Lord's Supper functions similarly. It is the covenant, family meal of the church. While baptism admits into the family, the Lord's Supper confirms. Regular participation in the Lord's Supper is a means by which our faith is nourished. Scripture is clear that you need to be able to discern and judge the meaning of the sacrament before coming to it (1 Cor. 11:27–32), which means a sincere profession of faith is a prerequisite for coming to the table.[5] Even children who have not been admitted to the table benefit from being present in the worship of the church when the sacrament is served. Beyond teaching, seeing the sacrament fuel the rest of the church helps whet children's appetite for deeper faith in Jesus.

How do our kids stay Christian? The same way they become Christians—through the grace of God. Prioritizing the means of communicating this grace builds and maintains our children's faith. Our kids stay Christian the same way they became Christians—through the regular gifts of God to his people, the family and covenant community of God. If we want our kids to stay Christian, we must prioritize those things using the normal means of grace. Family is divinely established in creation. Belonging and knowing God happen through family.

Chapter 2

FAITHFUL, FIRM, AND FUN
Parenting for Lifelong Discipleship

"Secularization Begins at Home." This was the alarming headline of a 2023 article by demographer Lyman Stone.[1] Though he expresses appreciation for the work of Burge, Davis, and Graham in *The Great Dechurching*, Stone convincingly argues that they missed a critical detail: Young adults who grew up Christian leave the church not because older generations fail to pass the baton but because Christian children under the age of twenty-two, and especially under the age of fifteen, never fully absorbed religious beliefs. Kids become secular not when they go to college or enter the workforce or move out of their parents' home but when they are children. "It should be clear that childhood, including before age 13, is the key battleground for religious formation, *not* adulthood," Stone says. "By the time a child goes to college, much of the religious question has already been settled."[2]

Stone contends that this secularization is occurring not because Christian parents have ceased to raise their kids as Christians over the last forty years but because of larger cultural changes in childhood socialization. Parental influence in general over their kids has declined as different forces (e.g., schools, day care, the internet[3]) take up larger chunks of kids' time and attention. Stone's solution is for parents to make a significant effort to recapture time and presence with their kids.

Both *The Great Dechurching* and Stephen Bullivant's *Nonverts* show that the way parents relate to their children is a significant factor in long-term faith retention. In the case of Bullivant's book, he demonstrates that "nonversion, like conversion, is nearly always a deeply personal decision grounded in the individual particularities of one's life experience and interwoven with one's relationship to parents, friends, and spouse."[4] This interweaving of "individual particularities" simply means that while each individual's deconversion is unique, the contextual framework remains steady: Children's relationships—above all, with their parents—inform how they relate to Christianity as adults.[5]

Additionally, a 2017 study by Lifeway Research focused on the church attendance habits of young adults who grew up Christian.[6] Overwhelmingly, the eighteen-to-twenty-two-year-olds who stayed in church did so because it was a habit formed in childhood that was an important aspect of their relationship with God. For those who dropped out of church, the routine of church attendance and religious practice was not ingrained in them, so a change in structure led to their declined attendance. The good news was that the young adults who returned to church primarily did so due to the encouragement of their family.

One of the key takeaways from this research is that churches should intentionally focus on the eighteen-to-twenty-two demographic as a turning point for long-term faith retention. However, the bigger picture presented by this research is that, as Stone noted, the battle for lifelong Christian discipleship is first fought in childhood, and even when young adults wander from the church, it is still the familial and parental connection that is most likely to draw them back.

These studies all confirm parents' outsized influence on their children's lifelong Christian faith and church attendance. On the positive side, good parental influence can solidify religious formation and even draw wandering young adults back to the faith. On the negative side, parental influence—even from parents who personally hold to Christianity and want their kids to do the same—can inadvertently redirect Christian kids away from faith. These studies confirm what sociologists of religion have known since the 1970s and support the case that secularism at home is responsible for the recent great dechurching.

What, then, is to be done? Is Stone correct in saying that parents need to recapture face time for religious formation of their children? This is where Adamczyk and Smith's work *Handing Down the Faith* is invaluable. Aware of the sociological data on parental influence, they set out to discover whether different parenting styles influence long-term faith retention. Their answer is a resounding yes. And not just the volume of parental presence with kids but the kind of parental interactions and styles matter a great deal.

Before any prescription on the church's ministry practices can be given, we need to understand the challenges involved in rising secularization at home and exactly what kind of parental style is necessary for cultivating a lifelong love of God. And the first step in doing that is to consider the pattern of faith found in the home.

Passing on the Christian faith from parent to child rests on two key elements. First, parents must possess a sincere faith—one that is not compartmentalized but woven into daily life. Second, they must embrace an authoritative parenting style that combines warmth with firm boundaries, rather than falling into authoritarian rigidity, permissiveness, or passivity. Pastors and church leaders must understand these principles to effectively disciple the next generation. This knowledge enables the church to accurately teach and equip parents, helping them cultivate a spiritually healthy home environment. Additionally, when parenting challenges arise, pastors must be able to discern the difference between spiritual health and dysfunction, diagnosing struggles with wisdom and offering the right medicine for the soul. Understanding what ingredients are most essential for childhood faith retention allows church leaders to shape ministry structures that prioritize the discipleship of families and children, ensuring that the church nurtures lasting faith in the next generation.

The Ordinary Rhythm of Genuine Faith

It's critical that parents teach the Bible and catechize their children in the articles of the faith, of course, but that alone is not enough to foster lifelong faith. Christianity is taught, not caught, but *how* it's taught affects whether kids hold on to it. Parents who successfully inculcate steadfast faith and love of God joyfully demonstrate the importance of their own faith on a daily basis. I'll always remember the time my toddler took some toast at dinner, ripped it in half, and joyfully said, "This is given for you." He intuited that the things that happened at church were naturally connected to the rhythms of our home life because of how seamlessly our faith formed our family.

The sincerity of a parent's faith matters immensely. Children are remarkably perceptive; they can discern whether faith is a central and authentic part of their parents' lives. Is their faith merely a compartmentalized activity relegated to Sunday worship and being around church people? Does faith inform the parents' decision-making? Is it a regular topic of conversation, woven into the fabric of daily life, or is it limited to Sundays and interactions with church friends? When parents talk about faith, is it canned and scripted or something that proceeds organically from their hearts? Is faith in Christ so fundamental to who they are that talking about and living life informed by it occurs naturally in the home? Do parents clearly love God? Do they delight in Jesus?

When parents tell *and* show what they believe, it communicates the reality and value of the faith to their kids. The parents who speak about Christianity only in terms of politics or holidays or as a foundation for good values communicate to their kids that faith is a limited utility that doesn't actually mean much to them. It's when faith in God sincerely permeates parents' lives that kids truly believe that it matters and retain it for themselves. Adamczyk and Smith found that parents whose faith is the warp and woof of their lives are the parents who pass along that faith.[7] As Smith says elsewhere,

> What can committed, religious parents do to increase their chances of raising children who, as young adults, believe

and practice some version of their religion? The first answer is simply to *be themselves*: believe and practice their own religion genuinely and faithfully. Children are not fooled by performances. They see reality. And when that reality is authentic and life-giving, they just may be attracted to something similar.[8]

After all, that concept of a life of faith is what God commands in the Shema (Deut. 6:4–9):

> Hear, O Israel: The LORD our God, the LORD is one. You shall love the LORD your God with all your heart and with all your soul and with all your might. And these words that I command you today shall be on your heart. You shall teach them diligently to your children, and shall talk of them when you sit in your house, and when you walk by the way, and when you lie down, and when you rise. You shall bind them as a sign on your hand, and they shall be as frontlets between your eyes. You shall write them on the doorposts of your house and on your gates.

The Shema is the proto-creed of God's people, the summation of who God is, how Israel relates to him, and what they are to believe. It is the distillation of the covenant: The Lord is God, he is *our* God, and we will love and follow him.

Sincere faith also necessitates that this faith has an object and definition to it. If parents are to pass it down, they must have beliefs they hold to. Parents who successfully hand down the faith to their children don't do so by vibe but by articulation. The Shema is a reminder that parents must believe in God as he has self-disclosed and share that belief with their children. The sincerity of parental faith should encompass not just lifestyle but specificity about God and our relationship to him. Kids will pick up on both lifestyle inconsistency and the genuineness of parental belief in doctrines. We are to teach our kids who God is and the good behavior that flows from that relationship.

The declaration of who God is moves seamlessly into the lifestyle of his people. They shall teach who God is to their children, and their belonging to him shall characterize all their lives, from their homes to their travel to their conversations to their mornings and evenings. Belonging to God and loving him with all our being ought to characterize the entirety of our lives.

The lifestyle application from the Shema could be updated to say, "The words of God will be on your heart, and you shall diligently teach them to your kids, talking about them around the house, when you're in the car on the way to school and running errands, when you're getting ready for the day at breakfast, and when you're settling down for the night and preparing to go to bed." And this command is not to the community in general but something to be carried out by parents. It is mothers and fathers who teach their children around the home as they live life.

Biblical wisdom teaches that when kids truly believe that faith matters to their parents, they believe it should matter to them, and they come to understand that faith in and love for God are not merely a set of theoretical doctrines but the essence of life itself. Faith that is passed on is not an accessory to the Christian life but its lifeblood.

One of the ways that churches can assist parents in passing down the faith is by encouraging them to take the airplane oxygen-mask approach. Parents should prioritize their own faith so they actually have something to pass along to their children in the first place. Parents need to invest in their own spiritual education and formation; doing so creates a spiritual trickle-down effect where they are equipped with the knowledge of the faith in order to pass it down. Discipling parents is the most important way that churches can ensure that the faith is passed down to their children, and discipleship efforts should prioritize this. For this reason there is great value in having younger parents attending adult discipleship classes rather than teaching Sunday school classes or the equivalent if it's an either/or circumstance.

My church once conducted a parenting class with the goal of encouraging young parents to effectively communicate their faith and spiritual habits at home. One of the teachers asked the parents what praying with their kids was like, and to their dismay they learned that the parents weren't praying with their kids because they didn't know how to pray themselves. Churches should disciple kids by prioritizing the discipleship of their parents in the basic content and habits of the faith so they have something sincere to shape their home lives.

When kids see that their parents are not engaged with the church's faith practices beyond Sunday worship, they internalize that faith practice is not really something for adults. It's always distressing when church members drop their kids off for some discipleship activity and, instead of sticking around for the companion discipleship for adults, leave to go grab a coffee. Or when activities like chores around the house, sports, or recreational pursuits consistently take priority for a parent over Sunday worship. When worship with the church is regularly eclipsed by more mundane activities in a parent's life, kids learn that faith is a lesser priority for adult life. Church and its community become something from which kids, like their parents, can graduate.

On the other hand, if parents are actively involved in things like adult education classes, midweek fellowship events, and small groups, it teaches kids that this firm connection to the church is the normal and best practice of the Christian life. Faith is a lifestyle, and when week-in-and-week-out Christianity is not just routine talking but practice in community, it teaches kids the importance of forging and maintaining these bonds with the body of Christ. One of the other benefits, especially with something like a community group, is that kids see that faith and church are not burdens but a community where fellowship and friendship are found. Their parents' lives joyfully orbiting the weekly routines of faith and community instills in kids the goodness of Christ and his church.

This is contrary to the common parental mantra "Do as I say, not as I do." Kids learn by imitation and word, and what parents really believe and value is taught by how they act. If parents constantly talk about the virtues of healthy living but are always eating junk food, their kids will follow their behavior, not their words. But if parents practice what they preach—exercising even when it's inconvenient, restraining themselves around junk food, and preparing healthy meals— their kids will hear about and receive a healthy diet and lifestyle, and they are far more likely to internalize those values and continue on healthily into adulthood.

Yet living out such an integrated faith requires intentionality. It begins with the parents' own relationship with God. Parents must cultivate their personal devotion through regular prayer, Scripture reading, and worship. This personal spiritual growth equips them to teach and model faith authentically. It also gives them the strength and wisdom to navigate the challenges of parenting in a way that glorifies

God. A genuine love for Jesus naturally overflows into conversations, decisions, and behaviors, creating an environment where faith is lived out, not just given lip service.

Pastors need to encourage parents to create intentional plans. I have found that asking parents over dinner or drinks what their plan is to intentionally strive for this integration is an invaluable spark to motivate them into action. Inviting parents to think aloud about how they're raising their kids along with how they're ensuring their faith is organically incorporated into the daily rhythms of their home is often a sufficient encouragement to begin or continue on in that endeavor.

This integration also involves practical steps. For example, parents can create habits of discussing spiritual truths during meals, car rides, and family gatherings. They can encourage curiosity and questions about God, making room for open and honest dialogue. Regularly praying together as a family and serving people in the community are other ways to demonstrate the relevance of faith in everyday life. Such practices reinforce biblical truths and show children that faith is more than inward and personal; it's also active and outward looking.[9]

Parents should aim to create a home atmosphere that reflects the joy and hope of the gospel. If faith is presented as a list of burdensome rules or a source of guilt, children may view it as oppressive rather than liberating. On the other hand, when faith is characterized by love, grace, and gratitude, it becomes attractive. Parents who delight in God and his goodness inspire their children to do the same. The gospel is, after all, good news—a message of redemption, transformation, and eternal hope. When parents embody this reality, they invite their children to experience the abundant life that Jesus offers.

What about parental failure? Hypocrisy is the stink of insincerity. One of the key findings in *The Great Dechurching* and *Handing Down the Faith* is that parental hypocrisy drastically undermines parental influence for faith retention. This is especially true when it comes to moral practice, when parents espouse one set of values and live another.[10] And how could it be any different? A sanctimonious parent whose behavior doesn't align with their words will teach their kids that those words are hollow. I can tell my kids every meal not to talk with food in their mouths or chew with their mouths open, but if I continue to do so myself, I show myself to be inconsistent and teach them that good table manners are unnecessary.

In the case of Christianity, moral hypocrisy seen up close by kids teaches them a more wretched truth: that the invocation of Christ is really a means to excuse sinful behavior. "My bad behavior is acceptable because I believe in God." When this happens, of course kids are going to see religion as a means for their parents to justify themselves without any change in behavior. And when they see good people in the rest of the world who don't require the invocation of Christian belief to justify their decent behavior, then faith seems to be both unnecessary and a barrier to moral living. Parental hypocrisy is a powerful teacher for secularism.

What then? Well, do parents acknowledge their shortcomings without excuse when they happen? According to Martin Luther, "When our Lord and Master Jesus Christ said, 'Repent' (Matt. 4:17), he willed the entire life of believers to be one of repentance." This is the first of Luther's Ninety-Five Theses, the opening salvo in the Protestant Reformation. All of the Christian life is to be one of repentance, of hating and turning away from sin and casting ourselves on the mercy of God in Christ, endeavoring to follow him in a new obedience. The gospel of grace is that we are sinners and God has lovingly provided us a Savior in Jesus Christ to save us from our sin. When we sin *and* confess our sins to him, "he is faithful and just to forgive us our sins and to cleanse us from all unrighteousness" (1 John 1:9). The Christian life is one of continual dependence upon God's gift of amazing grace in Jesus. We fail; God comes through. We stumble; he cleanses us. We sin; he forgives. And this posture should inform how we treat others. After all, we request in the Lord's Prayer that God will forgive us as we forgive others. We who have been transformed by God's grace and really grasp his mercy will extend forgiveness to others.[11]

The very fabric of the Christian life entails us acknowledging that we are sinners and still need God's help. The chief way in which Christian parents become hypocrites is not sinful behavior inconsistent with the faith but remaining unrepentant. When we sin, we are called to acknowledge it, admit we need God's mercy, and openly strive to follow him better. When this biblical imperative is practiced in the home, kids view parental shortcomings not as hypocrisy but as part of a faithful Christian life. A transparent faith, marked by repentance and reliance on God's grace, models the gospel in a way that resonates with children. One of the most effective ways for parents to tell and show the gospel is to be open with their kids that they too are sinners, though this is not an excuse for their behavior. They need Jesus, and God gives forgiveness through him to all who ask, even moms and dads.

This is hard for parents to do. Admitting we messed up to the kids we are supposed to be examples for is difficult; we feel like any admission of missteps calls into question our parental competency and moral authority. It's imperative that parents cultivate humility (the most vexing of virtues) in acknowledging sin and error. While the motivation should not be pragmatism, the payoff for the faith of children is massive. Nothing is as powerful as a parent admitting to a kid that they messed up and need their child's forgiveness. When kids understand that their parents are men and women under authority who answer to the same Lord as themselves, it teaches them not only that sin is bad but that we all need God's grace, even mom and dad. When they see their parents seek forgiveness, they see that the foundation of the gospel is real in their parents' lives. And when parents humbly ask their kids for forgiveness, the children realize that the hurts and wrongs done to them are valid, requiring redress, and that their parents acknowledge this. Most importantly, the kids grasp that it is not the exercise of power that defines their relationship with their parents, but the gospel. That, more than anything else, internalizes the Christian faith.

A Style of Parenting for Lifelong Faith

I grew up in the church, and when I think back to my friends who came up with me in the faith and recall their families, I remember people who were pious and loved God. I was in the homes of many of my church friends weekly and could see the way that faith was normal and part of the fabric of their lives. Yet, like so many of my peers who came of age during the great dechurching (and it was my generation, the Millennials, who truly led the mass deconversion), a significant portion of my friends did not remain Christian into adulthood. If ordinary, genuine faith on the part of parents is the key ingredient in childhood faith retention, what went wrong?

It is here that we turn to different styles of parenting. As every pastor knows (but most are too terrified to say for fear of the response), not every approach to parenting is good. There may be "no right way" to parent, but there are plenty of bad ways. Many Christian parents embrace an approach to raising kids that is downright counterproductive. Adamczyk and Smith set out to discover whether different styles made a difference in faith retention, and they found that mixed with faith being a normal aspect of daily, routine life, one parenting approach correlated with a significant rate of handing down the faith.[12]

They evaluated two key traits—parents' standards for their children and their warmth toward them—and analyzed how different combinations of these traits led to four distinct parenting styles. Parents who hold high expectations and clear boundaries for their kids and are warm, caring, and supportive in their interactions with them have an authoritative parenting style. This style, with sincere belief, is the kind that successfully passed faith on to their children. Clear expectations and warm affection powerfully influence children to embrace their parents' faith and practice as their own.

In contrast, other styles of parenting are actually damaging to a child's faith. Parents who are highly demanding and strict with their children but offer minimal emotional warmth and support follow an authoritarian parenting style. This approach leaves little room for bonding, engagement, or identification, making it harder for children to adopt their parents' values. The children of authoritarian parents hold their parents' expectations for them at arm's length, viewing them as belonging to the parents with little personal meaning for the kids themselves, and something to be freed from rather than internalized and embraced. On the other hand, parents who show abundant affection and empathy but set few boundaries or expectations exemplify what Adamczyk and Smith call a permissive parenting style, conveying to their children that their actions, including those related to religion, are of little consequence. Finally, parents who provide neither emotional warmth nor clear guidance adopt a passive parenting style, which similarly fails to establish a strong foundation for transmitting religious beliefs.

Four Parenting Styles

	Relationally Warm	Relationally Cold
High Standards	**Authoritative—** loving and engaged	**Authoritarian—** strict and distant
Low Standards	**Permissive—** affectionate and indulgent	**Passive—** disengaged and indifferent

It's evident why these alternative approaches tend to be less effective. In the case of my childhood peers, those who grew up Christian but walked away from the faith as adults were all parented by faithful people whose approach to child-rearing aligned with the latter three styles. The danger for children is parents who believe and either don't expect anything of their kids on the one hand or are tyrannical and overbearing about these expectations on the other.

This is also what Davis, Graham, and Burge found in *The Great Dechurching*.[13] The kids who held on to their faith were able to have conversations with their parents about it that were sincere (the parents knew their own faith and believed it) and humble (the parents were confident, not self-focused, defensive, or belligerent about the kids' questions and hesitations about the faith). Parents don't need to be sociologists or theologians but should know the content of their faith, believe it with sincerity, and be confidently humble.

Consider how these different styles might manifest in families. Authoritative parents, for instance, might set clear expectations about regular church attendance and participation in family devotionals while also taking the time to explain the reasons behind these practices. They might say, "We go to church together because it's a way to grow in our relationship with God and glorify him," while actively engaging their child in discussions about faith and listening to their questions with patience and empathy. These parents demonstrate both sincerity in their beliefs and a confident humility that encourages open dialogue about faith. A good gauge of how embedded these values are in the hearts of parents is how they treat church while on vacation. Rest from the routines of work and chores and school is wonderful, but when families go on a trip and take a break from church, the parents communicate that the value system of loving God with all their being and meeting with him in the regular routines of worship are less important than getting a respite from church. Attending church on vacation is a simple and clear way to express the centrality of the Christian faith in all of life, not something tedious from which we need an escape.

An authoritative parent knows what they believe and lives it out authentically, modeling a faith that is both approachable and inspiring. When the child resists attending church or expresses doubt, the parent responds with understanding, offering gentle correction and reaffirming their love. That understanding does not abolish the parent as an authority figure; after all, kids are to honor their parents in the Lord, but parents are to exercise that authority with sympathy.

In contrast, an authoritarian parent might enforce the same expectations but without the accompanying warmth or explanation. They could insist on church attendance as a nonnegotiable rule, stating simply, "Because I said so," and reacting to resistance with punishment rather than dialogue. This approach might achieve short-term compliance, but it risks fostering resentment or a sense of obligation devoid of personal conviction. When children voice doubts or hesitations, authoritarian parents might respond dismissively or even confrontationally, silencing questions rather than addressing them. Kids in this environment would view faith as a burden imposed by their parents, leading them to abandon it once they gain independence. Escape from the authoritarians means escape from their authoritarianism, which includes their religious beliefs and practices.

Many of my peers who walked away from Christianity grew up in homes like this. Their parents loved Jesus and wanted their kids to love him but didn't know how to manage their homes outside of the exercise of raw power. The parents look back and wonder what went wrong; they went to all the right activities, had all the right practices, believed all the right stuff, and enforced the rules. But they lacked humility, joy, and above all, patience.

Permissive parents, while well-intentioned, might prioritize their child's immediate happiness over long-term spiritual formation. They could say, "If you don't feel like going to church, that's okay," or avoid setting consistent expectations for spiritual practices. These kinds of parents often think they're letting kids figure out faith for themselves and giving them space without imposition so the kids will freely

choose it later. This comports with an American sensibil-
ity and also is often motivated by a fear that pushing their
kids will drive them away—the terror of becoming an authoritarian! In reality, the lack of enforced boundaries and
expectations inadvertently signals to their children that faith
is optional or unimportant. No good parent would have the
same approach with school or homework, and kids internalize the difference. Often this permissiveness stems from the
parent's lack of confidence in their own beliefs, which can
lead to an insincere or overly accommodating approach. As
a result, their children might grow up with a shallow understanding of religion, easily swayed by competing influences.

What I observe in my peers is that permissive parenting
works for faith transmission as long as the kid is naturally
interested in and disposed to Christian community and practice. But as soon as a kid in these families shows any kind
of resistance to or hesitation about Christianity, the parents
have no tools to guide or push them toward faith. Often there
is a course overcorrection, where they shift from permissive
to an unnatural authoritarianism that doesn't last since they
have no other tools or family culture to lean upon. This
whiplash and lack of sincerity further undercuts their kids'
faith retention.

Passive parents, on the other hand, might neither encourage nor discourage religious practices, leaving their
children without clear guidance. These parents are likely
to be "Chreasters": Christmas and Easter Christians whose
connection to the faith, which they may internally hold to
be sincere, is nominal in practice. These parents might avoid
conversations about faith altogether, due to either discom-
fort or a belief that their children should find their own
way. Without the framework of expectations or the warmth

needed to inspire trust and identification, children in passive households may struggle to see faith as relevant to their lives. This approach often conveys an unspoken message of indifference, leaving children feeling that faith is unimportant or irrelevant.

The fear of becoming an overbearing parent is pervasive. In a world where helicopter (or snowplow) parenting has become both too common and subject to vicious criticisms, parents are right to be cautious and not become authoritarian. However, one of the ways this has played out is that many American parents try to create distance and space between themselves and their kids. Especially following the stereotypes of kids growing up in the 1960s to 1980s— teens wanting to escape the watchful supervision of their parents and strike out on their own—the concern to not be smothering is sensible. Yet there is a difference between authoritarianism (ask any fifteen-year-old who feels like they live under a totalitarian roof) and involved parenting. Adamczyk and Smith have noted that the cliché of kids, even teens, who want space from their parents is no longer true,[14] if it ever really was. In other words, parents' involvement, excitement, support, engagement, and presence with their kids correspond to healthy children and kids who hold on to their faith. This effect is even true to a lesser extent with grandparents. Caring about a kid's life and making that care known by word and presence have a positive influence on their faith retention. Trying to back off so the kid can have their own faith space is not beneficial.

The distinction lies not in the parents' intentions—all four styles typically stem from a desire to do what is best for their children—but in the outcomes. Authoritarian parents may deeply value discipline and structure, believing these will instill strong moral character. Permissive parents may aim to nurture their children's individuality and autonomy, while passive parents may assume that avoiding pressure will lead to authentic belief. However, it is the authoritative parents who most effectively combine the strengths of these approaches: They provide structure and guidance without sacrificing the emotional connection that fosters trust and openness. Children in authoritative homes are more likely to internalize their parents' values because they experience those values within a loving, supportive relationship. For example, a child who sees their parents living out their faith through acts of service, kindness, and integrity—and who feels genuinely loved and valued within that context—is more likely to adopt those practices and beliefs as their own. Kids don't rebel against joy.

A good and hard area of application is school sports. These are fun for kids but are often scheduled for Sunday mornings. Yet a parent who wants faith to be central to their lives will hold a high standard for their family and not allow their kids to participate in activities that take them away from the life of the church. This is difficult and countercultural, potentially sacrifices other athletic opportunities, and risks the ire of kids who love the game. But it does set a high expectation for the family and, if upheld and conveyed in warm, understanding love, will effectively communicate the true importance of faith and practice from parent to child, even if it's not received that way in the moment. When parents are confronted with the choice of having kids at church or in some other activity, kids can tell which is of greater importance to that parent based on which activity wins out.

As I was growing up, my dad was supportive of us joining the Boy Scouts but was unwilling to let us be part of a troop that camped on Sundays unless there was a genuine worship service on the campout. My brothers and I didn't get what the big deal was; we'd be in church most Sundays, and camping was great. But my dad held the line. He understood that intentionally prioritizing something over the faith practices of our church would teach us that church attendance was optional if something better came along. You don't have to be a strict Sabbatarian to respect that, and while we didn't care for it at the time, over the long haul it was better for us (and we found a troop that met his standards). I respect my dad for lovingly holding us to those high standards.

Pastors need to be up-front with parents about this. We often fear hurting feelings or alienating people we want to be at our church, but we should be absolutely clear that parents are in charge of their kids and should set high expectations for them, even when the kids don't like it. I'm often asked by parents whether they should make their teenagers come to church, and the answer to that is "Yes!"—even if it means they're grumpy, they're missing out on sports or sleeping in, or they have to change their homework routine. And parents need to do this in a loving way that shows joy both for God and his worship and toward their children.

In our home, my wife and I practice this in several different ways. First, we try to have minimal rules and keep rules from piling up. Strangling childhood joy and freedom through household bureaucracy helps no one, and it's likely one of the things Paul had in mind when he told fathers not to provoke their children to wrath (Eph. 6:4). But what rules we do have we enforce relentlessly. These are the high boundaries we place upon our kids. We also committed that when we had kids we would bring them into our lives, not end our lives to revolve around them. Of course, parents need to make significant sacrifices to raise children and can't live as if they're still without kids. But they set the terms of the home and establish expectations. And those expectations are fused with warmth: "We will go to church, and isn't that great! You will do chores just like Mom and Dad, and isn't it great that you're contributing! You will do your schoolwork, and isn't it great that you get to talk to Mom and Dad about the cool things you're learning!" We have fun with our kids, tell them we love them, listen to what interests them, include them in what interests us, and above all let them know that we *like* them. Our kids will grow up knowing that we loved and sacrificed for them but also that we enjoyed them as individuals.

Authoritative parents might establish a routine of attending church as a family every Sunday, discussing the sermon over lunch, and encouraging their children to ask questions or share their thoughts. When a teenager expresses doubt about a core tenet of their faith, the parents respond not with anger or dismissal but with curiosity and respect, saying, "That's an important question. Let's talk about it together." This approach addresses the teenager's concerns while demonstrating that faith is a dynamic, living relationship rather than a rigid set of rules.

Now contrast this with an authoritarian household, where similar doubts might be met with statements like, "We don't question God in this house," or "You just need to believe." While the intention is to protect the child's faith, the effect is often the opposite: The kid feels invalidated and may distance themselves from both their parents and their parents' beliefs. Meanwhile, in a permissive household, the teenager's doubts might be met with indifference or overly accommodating responses such as, "Believe whatever feels right to you," which might leave the teenager feeling unmoored and unsure of what their parents truly value. In a passive household, the issue might not be addressed at all, leaving the teenager to navigate their doubts in isolation.

The key strength of authoritative parenting lies in its ability to integrate discipline with compassion, creating a nurturing environment where children feel secure enough to explore and embrace their faith. This approach mirrors the way God our heavenly Father is both just and merciful, upholding standards while offering unconditional love. When parents model this balance, they effectively pass on their faith and equip their children with the emotional and spiritual tools needed to navigate life's challenges. When kids know they are loved, they rise to the challenge of high expectations.

In short, children are more likely to embrace the religion of their parents when they enjoy a relationship with them that expresses both clear parental authority and affective warmth. These children know that their parents hold them to high standards precisely because they love them. They also know that when they fail to meet those standards, there will be consequences, but the parents will never withdraw their love and support.

By contrast, the other three parenting styles struggle to convey these messages as clearly, and the consequences for passing on religion are often seen in the next generation's diminished engagement with faith. Authoritative parenting, with its combination of clarity and compassion, is the most effective approach to nurturing a child's faith for a lifetime of Christian discipleship.

Chapter 3

LEADING BY EXAMPLE
Pastors as Discipleship Models

Each week, the young children of our church are invited to the front of the sanctuary for a lesson during the worship service. As I sit among them, I am keenly aware that every adult in the congregation is watching. In that moment, I strive to model authoritative pastoral leadership—relaxed and patient with their distractions, unbothered by their natural energy, yet taking their questions and diversions seriously. I engage them with warmth and joy while maintaining high expectations, ensuring they listen, respect one another, and uphold behavioral standards (no wrestling!). While the content of the lesson matters, its greatest value in this liturgical context is the model it provides for parents and grandparents on how to engage their own children with both love and authority. As a pastor, I seek to imitate Christ's own embrace of children so that, like Paul and Timothy, the church may imitate me in leading the next generation. It is a weighty duty, but it is central to the pastoral calling.

It's one thing to present biblical and sociological wisdom on the best style of parenting; it's another entirely for the church to promote that to parents. A quick Amazon search shows that there are over 60,000 books on parenting and over 10,000 for Christian parents. Only books about marriage outpace the output of parenting publications. We have no shortage of resources on the subject and quite a bit of dregs to be sorted through. There is biblical wisdom and insight on effective parenting, which the church should teach to its people.[1]

But beyond including teaching on the relationship between faith, covenant, parenting styles, and Christianity being passed along, there is little that the church can do in the classroom to teach parents. Yes, parenting classes or books can be helpful, but ministers cannot effectively encourage parents with words alone. In the same way that authoritative parenting works only if parents warmly model their sincere convictions throughout daily life, ministers must attend to the people of the church—including parents and especially children—with warmth and sincerity. Modeling a genuine and kind faith that is locked into God's Word is a prerequisite for any effective instruction on parenting styles.

The most effective way for churches to disciple parents in raising their children authoritatively is by having pastors, elders, and leaders serve as living examples for the congregation to follow. Before diving into specific staffing structures or discipleship programs, it is crucial for churches to establish the foundation of these role models. A church's greatest resource for shaping Christian families is its pastors and staff, who model authoritative leadership —high expectations paired with relational warmth, joy, and patience. Pastors demonstrate this first within their own families and then in their interactions with the children of the church. Additional staff members complement this role by modeling high standards and joy and intentionally equipping parents—mothers, fathers, single parents, and grandparents—to raise their children as faithful Christians. In doing so, churches prioritize the development of faithful families over reliance on programmatic solutions, which in turn sets up children for lasting Christian discipleship.

Pastors Are to Be Biblical Models

The Bible places significant emphasis on the qualifications for leadership within the church, specifically highlighting the importance of a pastor's or elder's parenting and home life. This is not a peripheral consideration but a central measure of suitability for ministry. As such, the parenting style of a pastor is effectively a job description for their pastoral role. The Scriptures affirm that how a leader manages their household reflects their character and provides a clear indication of their ability to lead and shepherd the church.

The apostle Paul, in his letters to Timothy and Titus, underscores the importance of household management as a criterion for church leadership. Paul writes in 1 Timothy 3:12, "Let deacons . . . [manage] their children and their own households well." Similarly, in Titus 1:6, he states, "[An elder must be] above reproach, the husband of one wife, and [whose] children are believers [or faithful] and not open to the charge of debauchery or insubordination." These passages make it clear that managing their household well, particularly their children, is essential for those aspiring to leadership roles such as pastor, elder, or deacon.

In Titus 1:6, the requirement for children to be "faithful" and not liable to accusations of debauchery or insubordination is the first in a series of qualifications that establish a leader as being above reproach. A godly and commendable candidate for ministry is one whose parenting is praiseworthy. This is why Paul says that a pastor is to manage their household well, "with all dignity keeping his children submissive" (1 Tim. 3:4). If a candidate for pastor cannot steward the familial blessings in their own home that God has given them, then how can they possibly be expected to oversee and steward the church, which is the household of God being given into their charge?[2]

Continuity between a pastor's home life and church life is an essential biblical principle. A pastor's parenting style—authoritative, authoritarian, permissive, or passive—often mirrors their style of pastoring. This biblical connection is not incidental but intentional, as the church itself is a true family. A pastor who leads their home with warmth, patience, humility, and joy fosters faith at home and is therefore more likely to foster a church environment that promotes godliness and faith.

The Bible illustrates this continuity further by emphasizing that a pastor's children are an indispensable part of the pastor's résumé. Their conduct, respectfulness, and faithfulness provide a tangible measure of the pastor's ability to shepherd effectively. This does not mean children of pastors are expected to be perfect but rather that their behavior reflects the spiritual leadership and intentionality of their parents.

The word *pista* in Titus 1:6 can be translated as "faithful" or "believers." Pastors cannot regenerate the souls of their children any more than they can save anyone else, and pastors' kids are worse off when their parents act like they're the Holy Spirit. Pastors and elders cannot unite their kids by faith to Jesus, so in that sense and for that reason, *pista* here cannot mean "having a saving faith in Jesus." But pastors, like any other Christian parent, can raise their children to be faithful participants and members of the covenant community. Are their kids living consistently with the message the parents are giving? If so, the church knows the pastors practice what they preach. This does not mean that pastors should raise their children to be insincere charades of Christians; rather, their kids should be raised to follow Christ in their behavior (submissive, not liable to accusations of rebelliousness and licentious living) because they are raised to love God (faithful). Do pastors raise the kids of the covenant to love the Lord who made the promise of salvation? Do the kids honor their parents in their behavior? Is the example that's set godly? When the kids sin and misbehave, how does the pastor respond? When the children imitate their parents, do they act how the church wants to act when they imitate their pastor?

The relationship between parenting and pastoring is reciprocal. Just as a pastor's parenting style influences their ministry, their pastoral leadership influences their parenting. This reciprocal relationship permeates the New Testament, which frequently calls church members to imitate their leaders in order to become more like Christ. Paul writes in 1 Corinthians 11:1, "Be imitators of me, as I am of Christ." He expands on this in Philippians 3:17 when he calls the church as brothers (a familial term!) to "join in imitating me, and keep your eyes on those who walk according to the example you have in us." It's no longer just Paul who should be imitated but also those who conform to the apostolic faith. Hebrews 13:7 instructs the church, "Remember your leaders, those who spoke to you the word of God. Consider the outcome of their way of life, and imitate their faith." The church is to hear the Word of God, imitate the faith of the leaders who speak God's Word, and judge the quality of their faith through how they live their lives. Follow the leader—and you can trust their words if their lifestyle is godly and worth imitating.

This call to imitation places a significant responsibility on pastors to serve as examples not only in their public ministries but also in their private lives and in the behavior of their kids. It's cliché but true: A child's conduct reflects upon their parents. How a pastor's kid behaves is a window into how the pastor parents. Paul's urging to Timothy to "set the believers an example" in his ministry (1 Tim. 4:12) is a reminder that all the qualifications for leadership in the church that he laid out several paragraphs earlier, including parenting, are to be practiced for the sake of setting an example of godly discipleship.

Likewise, 1 Peter 5:2–5 contrasts domineering leadership with example setting, emphasizing the importance of leading with humility and authenticity. In the context of parenting, this example setting includes demonstrating warmth, patience, humility, and joy. These qualities are not optional but essential, as they reflect the heart of God's shepherding care. Peter encourages pastors to be authoritative: having high standards and expectations (exercising oversight) with warmth (not domineering). Pastors shepherd like they parent. Parenting style is a nonnegotiable requirement on pastoral and elder job descriptions for candidates with children.

The biblical requirements for church leaders to manage their households well and have faithful, obedient, and respectful children serve a dual purpose. First, they ensure that pastors themselves embody the character and leadership needed to guide the church. Second, they provide a model for church members, particularly parents, to emulate.

Second Timothy 3:10–17 shows how the character of pastors and Christian leaders can establish patterns for the church to follow, particularly in passing the faith on to children. First, Paul commends Timothy for following his teaching, his conduct and aim in life, and his character of faith, patience, love, and steadfastness. Timothy conformed to his mentor's teaching not just because he was persuaded by Paul's doctrinal arguments but because he observed and followed his leader's character, just as the author of Hebrews instructed. And Paul doesn't list out stoic attributes or cold virtues, but patience and love.

Paul shared his beliefs with warm sincerity. Timothy bought into what Paul taught because of both the teaching's content and the teacher's character. And this led to him following Paul into persecution and suffering for the sake of Christ. Timothy shared the same goal in life as Paul—to know Christ and him crucified. When our faith is solidly grounded on that foundation, it produces a strength of character willing to share in the sufferings of this life as we follow Jesus. Timothy was sincerely and confidently committed to the doctrines of the faith as well as to the warmth of godly character.

Paul lists all of this to exhort Timothy to continue on in what he had learned and firmly believed so that the church, like Timothy, might have faith in Jesus Christ. This references primarily the biblical teaching of Paul; Timothy was to remain grounded in the faith and continue growing in his commitment to it for the benefit of the church. But it also references the conduct and character Paul described. Timothy was to imitate Paul in ongoing love, patience, steadfastness, and faith. Godly sincerity, confidence, knowledge, and faith go together with love and patience. Paul is telling Timothy to practice the example setting of 1 Peter 5:3—shepherd the church by the example of your teaching and warm character.

Timothy was in a position to be evaluated; the church was to consider his life for the strengthening of their faith. The character, fidelity, and godliness of pastoral examples should be evident when evaluated in order to motivate continued imitation, which in turn should instill confidence in the doctrine learned. Timothy's imitation of Paul was both for the sake of his own faith in Jesus and to pass on the faith through people in the church imitating him by following his character, listening to his teaching, and especially modeling his aim in life: to know God, glorify God, and enjoy God in and through Christ.

Paul is swift to remind Timothy, by recalling how Timothy came to faith, that it is not his character that saves people but faith in Jesus Christ in acquaintance with Scripture. The key to passing along the faith to our children is something Timothy started doing in childhood. The "whom" Timothy had learned the faith from is plural; it was not just Paul who had taught him but his family and community of faith. Timothy had first become wise to salvation as a kid. Now, even as a pastor, he is to continue not just in his imitation of Paul, his pastoral mentor, but also on the path he's been on since childhood.

Timothy's faith began as a kid and came through his knowledge of the Bible, and now he is to set the same model for the church. Just as Timothy imitated Paul, the parents and kids of the church are to imitate Timothy in familiarity with Scripture and follow the example of his godly character. And they can trust Timothy's teaching because of his godly character.

The kids of the church know that they can learn the Bible and grow to have the same faith as their pastor because the source of that faith is the same Scripture they have. Parents and grandparents of the church, like Timothy's own mother and grandmother, can see that it is possible to pass down the faith to their own kids. And just as Timothy continued to grow in his faith after reaching maturity, the parents and kids of the church can see an example of striving for continual growth. Timothy is to set an example to the church so that all its members, whether parent or child, can follow the teachings of God's Word to have the same aim in life. In all the ways that Timothy imitated Paul, he was to prepare to be imitated, and this would pass the faith along to the kids of the church.

Pastors are called to lead and equip others to lead in their homes. This is especially true for fathers, who bear a unique responsibility in biblical parenting (more on that later). If church leaders fail to model sincere, confident, and humble discussions of the faith, as well as a joyous approach to raising children, it becomes significantly harder for parents in the congregation to do the same. Pastors must intentionally model warmth, firmness, joy, and patience while taking proactive steps to teach these qualities.

The connection between parenting and pastoring has several practical implications for church leaders. First, it underscores the need for leaders to prioritize their family life. A pastor's primary call begins at home, where they have the duty and joy to raise their children. Neglecting this responsibility and blessing is a disservice to their children and compromises their credibility as a leader in the church.

Second, this connection challenges pastors to evaluate their parenting and consider how it aligns with biblical principles. Are they demonstrating the warmth, patience, and humility that reflect God's character? Are they setting an example of joyful, intentional parenting that inspires others to do the same? These questions are critical for ensuring that their leadership at home translates into effective leadership in the church.

Third, when potential candidates for church leadership are being considered, their parenting, their children's behavior, and how their adult children turned out should be key criteria in the assessment. Another key litmus test is how pastors and elders interact with kids who are not their own. Do they treat them as a nuisance—a bother to be avoided, shut up, or redirected elsewhere in the church? Or are kids treated with sympathy, joy, and respect? Patience is not just about tolerating something you wish to be over soon but also the practice of devoting attention to what is in front of you. When pastors interact with kids, are they patient? Are they giving the kids a focus that shows they care about what they have to say? Children, especially very little ones, are delighted when adults talk to them like they are also adults—not necessarily in vocabulary or subject matter, but taking what the kids are talking about just as seriously as they would with another adult. Headmaster Albus Dumbledore in the Harry Potter books and Bandit and Chilli, the parents in the *Bluey* television series, are great fictional examples of this. Fred Rogers exemplified it in real life. The range in personal styles captured in these characters shows that how adults should interact with children isn't a one-size-fits-all approach but rather patience embodied in different temperaments. Engage children with genuine esteem, fondness, and playfulness, and they will respond in kind. When parents respect children, engage in their interests, and delight in what they have to say, the kids listen to and ponder what adults tell them. Kids are people too!

This is a crucial way that pastors can model how to be authoritative parents and that a church can assess the quality of its leaders.

Family and Children's Ministry-Specific Staffing

If churches are going to hire staff who specialize in discipling families, the primary focus should be turning the hearts of children and parents toward each other. Cultivating an authoritative parental influence is critical, and this is done not first in the classroom or training seminars but through modeling. Family ministry and discipleship, while they can include parenting classes and things like Sunday school, should be about urging authoritative parenting and showing parents what it's like.

Malachi 4:5–6 speaks of the anticipated restoration of God's people. God, speaking through his prophet, promises to send Elijah prior to the great and awesome day of the Lord. Elijah will lead the people in repentance. This prophecy is the chief reason that Christ refers to John the Baptist, who prepared Israel for the coming of Jesus, as Elijah (Matt. 17:9–13). The restoration is characterized by Elijah "turn[ing] the hearts of fathers to their children and the hearts of children to their fathers" (Mal. 4:6). This is literally the last verse of the Old Testament, God's final word before the coming of Christ. Now, Malachi is primarily concerned with God's people turning back to the faith of their spiritual fathers (Jacob, Moses, Levi) and the covenant he made with them. This was the ministry of the first Elijah and of John the Baptist. Yet, in this prophecy of restoration, the hearts of the *fathers* are also being turned. Restored, faithful people of God are characterized by children who honor their parents and their parents' faith, and parents who love their children by passing down the faith to them. The restoration of God's people is a returning to their purpose established by his covenant. The fifth commandment that kids shall honor their father and mother is not just a standard but a promise. The God who covenants with his people will restore them to this blessed condition, and their lives will be characterized by living out the summons of the Shema. This is what it means for their hearts to be turned to each other: affectionate sincerity, love for each other as people, and commitment to the covenantal faith to which they are bound.

The work Elijah and John the Baptist were called to is the same work the church is commissioned with: to lead the people of God in setting their hearts on him and, by lovingly following Jesus, to obey him by setting their hearts on each other. The mission of the church is to lead Christian children and parents to set their hearts on each other. Any staffing or programmatic organization should aim for that. Is the core of the church's approach to family discipleship and ministry about turning the hearts of children and parents back to each other?

Shame is a powerful motivator, but its power often leads to harm when wielded carelessly. Parents in particular face immense pressure to "get it right," surrounded by endless debates over the right and wrong ways to raise their children. Some parents internalize this pressure, conforming to whichever standard is most loudly advocated at the moment, while others harden themselves, refusing to accept any critique of their parenting. However, Christ came to save us from sin and the destructive weight of shame. Shame, when used as a tool to influence behavior, is often counterproductive.

Early in my ministry, I learned this truth the hard way. In an effort to encourage high school students to deepen their faith and connection to the church, I took a shame-based approach, focusing on their shortcomings and urging them to improve. One perceptive senior pushed back, saying that I was using "shame-based discipleship," and she was right—I had been trying to motivate through guilt. That experience taught me a valuable lesson: While failure is real and often needs addressing, joy is a far more effective and enduring motivator. Encouraging people to pursue the better path because it is worth it resonates far deeper than trying to shame them out of their failures.

All too often, we carry shame for things that should never have caused us shame. At its core, shame is a response to behavior, prompted by either external criticism or our internal moral compass. When we do bad things, we are guilty of the wrong and *should* feel ashamed for that. Yet, for parents, navigating this emotional terrain is uniquely challenging. The overwhelming advice of parenting books and the heated debates about parenting style and effectiveness create a cacophony of pressures, which, coupled with the irreversible nature of parenting decisions, can leave many parents feeling paralyzed by regret. For those who carry shame over past mistakes, learning about wiser parenting styles for handing down the faith often compounds their feelings of failure. In the church context, this challenge is particularly acute.

When children's ministry shifts its focus from teaching kids to equipping parents, it is sometimes perceived as a critique of the parents' past efforts rather than an invitation to grow. Even the idea that parents bear the primary responsibility for their children's faith can feel overwhelming, leaving them burdened by a sense of failure. Without careful guidance, such messaging can unintentionally foster despair instead of hope.

A strategic shift in ministry philosophy requires thoughtful programming and a pastoral approach rooted in encouragement and grace. Effective pastoral modeling begins with recognizing that parents (especially single parents) and grandparents are navigating complex lives filled with pressures from work, relationships, and society. They need support, not criticism, as they strive to nurture faith in their children.

Churches must prioritize creating an environment where parents feel equipped, encouraged, and empowered. Language matters deeply here. Instead of platitudes that can feel hollow, such as "You're doing enough," it is more meaningful to say, "Love covers a multitude of parenting missteps." Kids knowing their parents love them is far more powerful than getting the best balance of firmness and warmth, and it's a balm for the deepest parental hurts and shame. Pastoral leaders can further foster this sense of belonging by being transparent about their own struggles in guiding their families spiritually. By modeling vulnerability and dependence on God, they can encourage parents to embrace growth over perfection, not just for themselves but in how they relate to their kids. This kind of modeling can happen in the pulpit, of course, but best occurs through interpersonal relationships. If a church is going to staff a family ministry position, they need to hire someone with the emotional bandwidth to be involved in the life of parents as both a friend and a mentor, and who is capable of recruiting seasoned parents in the church to craft a culture where this can happen naturally. This approach also helps new parents feel less like amateurs being corrected and more like practitioners learning from compassionate veterans.

Equally important is the way correction and accountability are handled. When encouraging parents to take a more active role in their children's faith development, church leaders should emphasize hope and opportunity, not guilt. Feedback should be framed in terms of possibilities: "Imagine what God could do in your child's life if you prayed together regularly," rather than, "You need to pray with your kids more." This reframing shifts the focus from what parents lack to what they can gain.

The role of joy cannot be overstated here. Joy is contagious, and when church staff and volunteers model an attitude of celebration, parents are more likely to feel inspired rather than burdened. Celebrate small wins, like the parent who tries a family devotional for the first time, the grandparent who starts praying with their grandchildren, or the Sunday school teacher who encourages a shy child to open up. These moments of affirmation remind families that faith formation is about progress, not perfection.

One challenge often overlooked in family ministry is engaging parents whose children are already grown. For these parents, messages about equipping families can feel irrelevant or even be painful reminders of missed opportunities. Pastors and church staff must acknowledge this reality with compassion while finding ways to involve these individuals in the life of the church. One approach is to encourage them to mentor younger parents. Their experiences—both successes and failures—can provide invaluable perspective and encouragement to those still in the thick of raising children. Hosting intergenerational gatherings or small groups can facilitate these connections, creating a culture of mutual learning and shared wisdom. All of these are ways that staff can teach parents to put on their own oxygen masks first so they can lead their kids.

Ministering to Fathers

When it comes to faith transmission and authoritative parenting, it is vital to recognize the unique roles that mothers and fathers play. Modeling is a key part of mentoring, and both parents require distinct guidance to fulfill their God-given roles effectively. This is especially true of fathers, who occupy a pivotal position in shaping their children's spiritual and emotional lives. This is not merely a matter of teaching doctrine or acting as "deputy pastors" at home; it is embodying a relationship that fosters warmth, joy, and encouragement—qualities that profoundly impact children, especially teenagers.

The relationship between fathers and their children significantly influences teen mental health.[3] Research consistently highlights the importance of paternal involvement in promoting emotional stability and resilience. Teenagers in particular thrive when they experience a secure and positive bond with their fathers. A dad's presence as a source of joy, encouragement in risk-taking, and support during failure fosters a foundation of trust and confidence. These qualities go beyond surface-level engagement to create a deep connection that resonates into adulthood. Fathers who actively demonstrate warmth and a willingness to delight in their children—not merely manage them—build an environment where faith can flourish.

What makes this bond even more remarkable is its impact on faith transmission. The quality of the father-child relationship is one of the most predictive factors in a child's likelihood of embracing their father's faith.[4] This does not diminish the critical role of mothers, but it does underscore the irreplaceable contribution of fathers as relational anchors.

However, it's crucial to note that this influence does not stem primarily from fathers taking on the role of spiritual leader at home. While teaching the faith and leading devotions are valuable, they are secondary to a father's ability to model God's love through their actions. Dads who engage with their children as individuals to delight in—not as projects to complete—build up their children's confidence and identities. When dads foster an atmosphere of joy, excitement, and care, they exemplify God's fatherly love in a tangible way. According to author Vern Bengtson, "Fervent faith cannot compensate for a distant dad. . . . A father who is an exemplar, a pillar of the church, but doesn't provide warmth and affirmation to his kid does not have kids who follow him in his faith."[5] Dads influence their kids regardless of their intent, and it is warmth and affection before theology and passion for God that will encourage his kids to follow in faith.

The church has a crucial role in equipping fathers for this task. Before they consider hiring a youth pastor, children's ministry coordinator, or family ministry director, the church should consider hiring a men's and dads' pastor. Direct communication is an essential part of this mentoring process. Many fathers may feel ill-equipped or unsure of how to express love and encouragement to their children effectively. The fear of shame can drive pastors to downplay the importance of this, but men respond well to direct calls to action.

A patriarch in my church recently shared how he had been nominal in his faith while his wife was very much committed, even though he wanted his kids to grow up Christian. One Sunday when he happened to attend church, the pastor said that kids whose dads did not attend worship or own their own faith were not likely to remain Christian. That simple, implied challenge was the kick in the pants he needed, and he committed to genuinely investing in his faith for the sake of his kids. And dads who do that not only bless their children but encounter Jesus themselves.

In the broader context of church ministry, fostering a culture that supports fathers in their role is vital. This should be absolutely intertwined with any adult or men's ministry approach to discipleship.[6] Ultimately, the goal is to help fathers see their children as God does: not as burdens or problems to solve but as beloved individuals to cherish and nurture. By equipping fathers to model this perspective, the church can empower families to transmit their faith more effectively, ensuring that the next generation experiences the transformative power of God's love firsthand.

Ministering to Mothers

Mothers play an integral role in the transmission of faith within the family, and their influence shapes the religious and spiritual trajectory of their children in unique and powerful ways.

One of the most significant ways mothers influence faith transmission is through their role in selecting and shaping the family's religious practices. Mothers often take the lead in choosing a church or faith tradition, either by asserting their preferences or by selecting an option that aligns with their husband's willingness to participate. This practical decision-making helps establish a foundation for the family's religious identity and creates an environment where faith can be nurtured. In many cases, fathers follow the spiritual framework set by mothers, underscoring the critical role of maternal leadership in this area. A 2023 study reconfirmed what sociologists have known since the 1970s—that children generally remain in the same faith tradition as their mothers.[7] Mom picks, dad energizes.

Warmth is another hallmark of a mother's influence on faith. While warmth is essential for all parental relationships, a mother's unique ability to create an atmosphere of emotional safety often allows children to engage more openly in conversations about faith. This is especially significant when fathers, for various reasons, are less approachable or expressive regarding spiritual matters.[8]

During a child's formative early years, mothers are typically the primary influence in establishing religious practices. From teaching children to pray to modeling daily devotional habits, mothers lay the groundwork for lifelong spiritual disciplines. This foundational role introduces children to the basics of faith as a sense of consistency and purpose is instilled in their spiritual lives.

While fathers undeniably play a crucial role in faith transmission, it is often mothers with whom children feel most comfortable discussing spiritual matters. This is not to suggest that mothers act solely as a backup when fathers are

absent or disengaged. Rather, maternal influence is a significant and independent force in its own right. Mothers provide
a relational depth that complements the contributions of
fathers, offering children a fuller and more balanced understanding of faith. Modeling authoritative parenting styles
for mothers in particular best occurs through the networks
of women and moms already in the church, especially older
women (see Titus 2:3–4). Establishing these networks is the
most effective route for churches to disciple moms to raise
godly children.

Speaking the Faith at Home

If secularism at home is to be avoided, then parental warmth
and sincerity need to be met with knowledge—parents need
to teach the actual contents of the Christian faith at home.
The premise of the Shema is that parents are not babbling
about a genericized sense of faith; they are talking about
the concrete specifics of God's covenant. Parents need to
pass down not vibe but a belief, and if kids are to be Christian, then parents need to be provided with the tools to do
that. This is the picture of Proverbs 22:6, put into practice
by Timothy's mother and grandmother. They acquainted
Timothy with the sacred writings and the doctrines of God
and thereby trained him up in the faith. The Protestant tradition historically prized not only personal devotions and corporate worship but also family worship—a daily time when
parents and children read God's Word, discussed it, prayed
together, and sang. The wisdom of our forebears bore fruit,
and following that wisdom is key to passing down the faith.

Demographer Lyman Stone discovered that if we want
our kids to stay Christian, we must double down on home

discipleship.[9] The church needs to encourage these practices at home if families want their kids to stay Christian. Kids love it when families sing together, especially when there is energy to the music. They are invigorated when dads and moms get into the music. Stylistically, sea shanties are good examples of family-friendly styles of music that infuse joy into the home regardless of the kids' ages.

It is here that the joyfulness of dads is key. If family worship is treated as another homework assignment or chore, then kids will hate it, especially when it comes to music and the vulnerability of prayer. But if dads are excited and joyful, the kids will be also. Churches can help by providing guidance and recommendations on the content of family worship. The number of family devotionals is overwhelming, and giving members of the church something accessible to guide them is invaluable, especially with the range of life stages of kids.[10] Parents having tools to consistently present the content of the Bible and doctrines of the faith is a key way the church can equip them. Life is busy, and different seasons make this more or less doable.

Pastor and author Kevin DeYoung once commented at a Together for the Gospel conference that the important thing is not rigid regularity in family worship, but that if family worship is a consistent feature that continues to pop up and is embedded in the life of the family—even if different seasons submerge it from time to time—it remains effective for passing down the faith. He's right. Family worship doesn't need to be elaborate; its value for faith transmission is in providing an opportunity to hear God's truth and respond to it. One of the ways my parents accomplished this when I was being homeschooled was beginning each morning session with a devotion and a time for us kids to pray for people in need in our community. Another good example of this is from the parents of my childhood friend Andrew. Toward the end of dinner, whether their kids were toddlers or in high school, Steve and Kelly read a brief devotional or reflection on Christian faith in the world (often the intersection between faith and science), and then the family together discussed it. When friends came over, they kept up the practice and invited us into it.

It's easy for Christians to fall prey to the fear of being perceived as hokey and weird in this area. There's a great scene in the sitcom *Arrested Development* where teenager George Michael recalls the creepy Christmas party at his religious girlfriend's home, and the camera cuts to a small group of people awkwardly singing off-key about the blood of Jesus. George Michael was negatively contrasting that gathering with the parties hosted by his wildly dysfunctional family. The viewer is left with no doubt that the singers at the Christmas party were sincere in their faith, yet we're afraid of the world thinking of us like that: oblivious to how ridiculous and out of touch we really are.

The faith of the Flanders family in *The Simpsons* is played for laughs because they are so zealous, all-consuming, and oblivious to their own overbearing awkwardness. No one wants to come off as chumps. Interestingly, *The Simpsons Movie* inverts this by redeeming Ned, the patriarch of the Flanders family. Bart Simpson becomes exasperated with his negligent dad and turns to Ned, who becomes a father figure to him. Ned never acts any different than normal or ignores his own children, but he allows Bart to join in with the family and shows genuine care for him. It's only when Homer provides the fatherly attention that Bart needs that his son's affection reverts back to him. *The Simpsons* understood that even though the Flanders family's caricature of faithfulness is good for playful mockery, the sincere, routine faith and fondness of their family is actually good—even better than the alternatives. It's only when Homer begins acting like Ned that he becomes a good dad.

The world may scoff at the apparent awkwardness of a family who unabashedly makes Christian faith the fabric of their life, but that sincere, confident, and warm family is actually admirable and better for everyone. Don't let the fear of ridicule undercut commitment to a routine Christian faith. The church can support, equip, and teach, but the home is the front line of a discipleship that lasts a lifetime. A routine Christian faith that shapes the rhythm of a family's life isn't an extra task but the mission of parenting. The church's call is to empower the parents for that mission.

Chapter 4

INCORPORATION, NOT ACCOMMODATION

The Power of Corporate Worship

If you want kids in your church to grow up Christian, then include them in the church's corporate worship.

This is one of the greatest influences on faith retention, though not nearly as high as direct parental and family influence. But these two things go hand in hand. If children are segregated from the rest of the church in worship, including their parents, kids in their formative stages don't see how much their parents value worship. Rather than accommodating children, churches ought to strive for their incorporation.

Adamczyk and Smith found that children who maintained their parents' faith were included in the liturgical activities of their worshiping communities.[1] This is the first of the important ways that parents use channels to pass along their faith. "Channeling" is a sociological term describing parental use of programs, institutions, and activities (e.g., after-school sports) to express and implement their values and pass along their principles and traditions. For handing down the faith, the two most critical channels are church worship and community.[2]

American churches are great at accommodating children. Nurseries, Sunday school, youth group, and children's church are just some of the myriad ways that churches work to accommodate children so that both they and their parents can freely attend worship services. This spirit of accommodation is well-intentioned but, when it comes to ensuring that kids grow up Christian, misguided. Incorporation of children into the worship of the church, rather than a siloed accommodation, should be the church's strategy.

Parents prioritizing corporate worship with and in front of their kids communicates the value of faith to their children by actions, not just words. Parents attending worship services alongside their children (the channel) teaches both that parents walk the walk enough to set aside time and devotion to a public expression of faith, and that this isn't something reserved just for one generation (either children's church or "big" church) but for all followers of Jesus.

Rather than merely accommodating children in church life, pastors and congregations should strive for their full incorporation into its gathered worship. Worship is not an experience reserved for adults; it is the shared life of God's people, and children are no exception. Including kids in the worship of the church is a vision that needs pastors and congregations alongside parents. Pastors and church leaders must recognize that what parents truly love, they pass down to their children—including a love for worship. Fostering that love is invaluable for lifelong discipleship. Scripture provides both principles and examples that affirm the presence of children in corporate worship, yet many churches hesitate due to common obstacles and objections.

Worship Models a Contagious Love

I've been a loyal fan of the Minnesota Vikings since I was four or five years old, through gut-wrenching seasons and multiple state moves. But my dad and brothers switched their team loyalty to the Dallas Cowboys after moving to Texas, and my in-laws, who are from the Lone Star State, are also committed Cowboys fans. Now I live in Philadelphia, and my oldest son, who knows nothing else, loves the Eagles as well as his grandpas' Cowboys (try reconciling that one). Yet Matthias's favorite team is the Minnesota Vikings. Why? Because his dad loves them and gets excited whenever they play.

Parents have no problem passing down their sports loyalty. Their kids become fans of teams or schools long before they can reason through which team they should support. The love of the team is taught by their parents' enthusiasm and caught by the children. And when parents watch games, they don't send the kids out of the room or to a different, age-segregated section of the stadium; they watch together. Just because the kids don't understand all the rules doesn't mean they're not really rooting for their team. Their participation in sports as spectators gives them ownership of the team.

Worship is the same. When children witness their parents worshiping and worship God alongside them, the gospel is taught and kids catch the love of God. Fathers and mothers worshiping God with their children is the demonstration that what is said the rest of the week has merit, that it really is believed. Otherwise it's like talking up a team but never watching the game. Kids' participation in the worship of the church gives them a loyalty to the faith, not as spectators but as worshipers.

Consider for a moment the profound impact of shared experiences. Sporting events capture this perfectly. A family gathered around the television, donning team jerseys and cheering in unison, creates bonds that endure for a lifetime. Even if a child doesn't grasp the intricacies of the game—the strategies, penalties, or rules—they know this: *They belong.* They are part of something bigger than themselves, something exciting and deeply meaningful. Over time, that sense of belonging and shared enthusiasm shapes their identity. They become Vikings fans or Cowboys fans because it's more than a preference; it's a legacy woven into the fabric of their family life.

In the same way, worship is a shared experience that can leave an indelible mark on a child's heart. It's more than singing hymns or listening to sermons; it's about participating in a covenantal act of devotion to God. When children see their parents singing joyfully, praying sincerely, and engaging wholeheartedly in the worship of God with the rest of the church, they learn that worship is not merely a ritual but an expression of genuine faith. They catch their parents' enthusiasm, just as they would for a favorite team, and it shapes their spiritual identity. Of course, this requires parents to actually be enthusiastic and sincere in their faith. One of the benefits of children participating in corporate worship is that kids are worshiping alongside both their parents and other adults (and kids) of the church. When mom or dad is less than enthusiastic about being there, the fellowship of the saints provides a safety net of sorts in communicating the value and joy of worshiping God together.

This analogy also highlights the importance of inclusion. Imagine the absurdity of a parent telling their child, "You're too young to watch the game with us. Go play in another room." Such an approach would sever the child's connection to the family's shared passion and diminish their sense of belonging. Similarly, when children are excluded from worship or relegated to separate spaces during church services, they miss out on the formative power of worshiping alongside their parents. By involving children in worship, even if they don't fully understand every aspect, we communicate that they are valued members of the church.

It's worth noting that children's understanding of faith grows through observation and participation. Just as a young fan's knowledge of football deepens with each game they watch, a child's grasp of the gospel expands through repeated exposure to the rhythms of worship. They may not understand every theological nuance, just as they may not grasp every play on the field, but they are learning. They are absorbing truths about God's love, grace, and majesty through the actions and attitudes of their parents.

This is why consistency matters. Just as a parent's unwavering support for their team demonstrates loyalty, a parent's faithful commitment to worship sets an example of spiritual steadfastness. Children notice when their parents prioritize worship, even when it's inconvenient or challenging. They see that faith is not merely a Sunday morning activity but a core part of life. And as they grow, they are more likely to emulate that commitment, making it their own.

In the end, both sports fandom and worship boil down to love. Love for a team draws a family together in celebration and camaraderie, while love for God unites a family in reverence and adoration. By modeling love—whether for a football team or the Creator of the universe parents pass down a legacy that shapes their children's hearts and lives. We believe this when it comes to something as trivial as sports, so we should certainly act and believe it when it comes to Jesus Christ. Worshiping together as a family is a profound declaration of what truly matters. The value of this family dynamic in worship is crucial for lifelong discipleship, and pastors and congregations should strive in light of that to encourage kids and parents to be together in worship.

And, of course, this is what we see in Scripture.

Biblical Pictures and Principles for Children in Worship

When it comes to including children in the corporate worship of the church, three different groups need to be persuaded of the value of the practice: pastors, parents, and congregations. Sociological data is helpful and interesting, but the biblical witness grants a firmer foundation from which to begin.[3]

Now, nowhere does the Bible expressly state, "You shall include everyone over the age of two in your 9:30 Sunday morning service." But the Bible does provide pictures and principles for how we should think about the inclusion of children in the church's worship. We are actually given very few examples of corporate worship in the Old Testament, but there are several important assemblies recorded that give us a good glimpse.

The book of Deuteronomy is a rearticulation of God's law prior to Israel entering the promised land. It includes a summation of the covenant terms of God's relationship to his people and their obligation to him, and as part of this review, Moses assembles all the people for the reading of the law. Deuteronomy is actually three different sermons from Moses, with him reading the law to the people, concluding with an epilogue.[4] The second sermon occupies most of the book—Deuteronomy 5–28 is one long scene,[5] with Moses going into detail about God's law. The start of the third sermon, Deuteronomy 29–30, presumes Israel's familiarity with all that Moses had preached earlier (29:9 says, "Therefore keep the words of this covenant"), because it's a sequel. And in 29:10–11 Moses states, "You are standing today, all of you, before the LORD your God: the heads of your tribes, your elders, and your officers, all the men of Israel, *your little ones*, your wives, and the sojourner who is in your camp" (emphasis added). All the people of Israel are congregated before Moses for his exposition of God's law, including even the smallest Israelites. And since this is the third installment in Moses's sermon series, there is no reason to presume that the composition of the congregation here is abnormal—the little ones are present for the gathered reception of God's Word all throughout Deuteronomy, even that mammoth twenty-four-chapter-long sermon.

This expectation of a comprehensive gathering of the covenant people is repeated with greater clarity in Deuteronomy's epilogue. Moses writes all this law and gives it to Israel's ministers (31:9). He instructs them to have all of Israel assemble[6] every seven years for the Feast of Booths celebration (v. 10), which is a commemoration of God's provision for his people in the wilderness. In this assembly the law is to be read to the people, and all the "men, women, *and little ones*, and the sojourner" (v. 12, emphasis added) are to be gathered to hear it, especially so that the children who may not know God's Word may hear and "learn to fear the LORD your God" (v. 13).

When the law of God, his Word, is read to the assembled people of God, all his people, including the littlest ones, are expected to be present. And the primary beneficiaries of this practice are the children! In the case of the Feast of Booths, on the one hand this is something like a fail-safe, to ensure that all the kids of Israel are learning God's Word. The law's expectation was that parents were teaching their kids at home, but even in ancient Israel parents weren't always the best at following through on spiritual nurture. On the other hand, the clear presupposition on Moses's part is that knowing God ("learn to fear the LORD your God") is something that comes by God through his Word. Faith comes by hearing, and hearing through the Word of God is not a concept introduced in the New Testament but is present in God's law. And God uses the exposition of his Word to produce faith in children who are otherwise ignorant of their Lord.

Children's participation in the congregated worship of God was not limited to these big gatherings. Whenever Israel was to assemble to worship and feast before God according to his appointment, it was to be done with the whole household (Deut. 12:5–7; 14:22–26; 15:19–20).

The presence of children in Old Testament worship continues throughout Israel's history. After Israel's failure at Ai, Joshua assembles the people to renew their covenant with God. "There was not a word of all that Moses commanded that Joshua did not read before all the assembly of Israel, and the women, and the little ones, and the sojourners who lived among them" (Josh. 8:35).

Jehoshaphat is a king of Judah who reforms the nation and leads them in turning back to God. In preparation for battle, Jehoshaphat assembles all of Judah before God at the temple in Jerusalem. He stands before the congregation and leads them in prayer, and "all Judah stood before the

LORD, with their little ones, their wives, and their children" (2 Chron. 20:13).

When reforms again take place under Josiah, he assembles all the people of Judah and all the residents of Jerusalem before the temple to hear the reading of the book of the covenant in accordance with the law, and all the people are present, "both small and great" (2 Kings 23:2). While children are not specifically mentioned here, the particular use of the term "small" as part of the catchall for the composition of an assembly—done in accordance with the law for the purpose of conforming to the law—indicates that the small, insignificant residents of Jerusalem present for the reading of the covenant included the covenant children. "Small" here corresponds to the "little ones" of Deuteronomy 31:12.

When Ezra and Nehemiah lead reforms of postexilic Israel, they assemble the people to renew the covenant and hear God's Word. In Ezra's case, after a dour confession of sin, "a very great assembly of men, women, and children, gathered to him out of Israel" (Ezra 10:1). The kids are present even for the emotionally hard times of worship. In the book of Nehemiah, Ezra appears again to read the law of Moses to the assembly, "both men and women and all who could understand what they heard. . . . And he read from it . . . from early morning until midday, in the presence of the men and the women and those who could understand" (Neh. 8:2–3). This is the first time a lower age limit is indicated, in that all the kids capable of understanding the reading of the law are present. But Nehemiah is silent on whether even younger children who couldn't understand are also present. The length of the service is not tailored to wiggly people with short attention spans but lasts for at least several hours. The kids are in attendance for the whole thing: "The ears of all the people were attentive to the Book of the Law" (v. 3). When the new wall of Jerusalem is finally completed, there is a worship service of consecration, and Nehemiah specifically notes that "the women and children also rejoiced" (12:43).

Finally, when the prophet Joel urges the people of Israel to repent, he commands them to "call a solemn assembly; gather the people" and to "assemble the elders; gather the children, even nursing infants" (Joel 2:15–16). The framework assumed by Joel and intelligible to the Israelites is that gatherings to worship God and to meet him on his covenant terms includes the children of God's people, even down to little babies. In the Old Testament, whenever the composition of the assembly to worship God is detailed, kids are always included.

The New Testament never provides a similar detailed composition of the church but operates with this Old Testament framework. For instance, the letters of Paul were part of the reading of Scripture in the church's worship (Acts 15:21; Col. 4:16; 1 Thess. 5:27; 1 Tim. 4:13; 2 Pet. 3:15–16), and twice he directly addresses children. The first time is in Ephesians 6:1–3, where he notably instructs children to obey their parents in the Lord. Paul does not say, "Parents, tell your kids to obey you in the Lord," but writes directly to the kids. When he tells them this, he is reminding them that their first motivation for obedience to their parents should be their belonging to God; because they belong to God, they should obey the authority he has established over them. This rhetorical device works only if Paul believes the children present for the reading of the letter are part of the covenant community already. Similarly, when he says that kids should recall that the fifth commandment is part of a list and the first one "with a promise" (v. 2), he is assuming their familiarity with the Ten Commandments (i.e., the law of Moses), something that was to be communicated in the worship of the church.

Paul makes a similar exhortation in Colossians 3:20, the second time he addresses children directly. This comes right after he encourages the church to "let the word of Christ dwell in you richly" (Col. 3:16). This is true for the children of the church as well. They should be taught and admonished by, and teach and admonish, one another and the whole church "in all wisdom, singing psalms and hymns and spiritual songs." Here, Paul's expectation is that the kids who heard his letter read in the church's worship are letting God's Word dwell in their hearts and are able to fulfill the command to teach and sing in all wisdom with the rest of the church precisely because they are part of that community.

So why is this the case? Why is something that is counterintuitive to our modern approach to children, discipleship, and worship treated as normal in Scripture? Part of the disconnect arises from the way we tend to think of worship—as an education by the passing along of information. When worship is first thought of as the transferal of information, then having young children present runs counter to our programmatic age. But when worship is properly understood as a covenantal encounter between God and his people, then including his youngest saints in worship makes complete sense.

The church is the community bound together through its covenantal union with God, and that bond is expressed in worship, where the people of God approach him and are met by him in the context of the relationship that he established and guaranteed by his Word. Most of the foregoing Old Testament examples of special assemblies are instances of either God reaffirming his covenant ("Here's the relationship

I have established with you by my Word") or renewals of the covenant by his people ("We have failed the relationship you have established with us, but by your grace we pledge to recommit ourselves to you on your terms"). And the children are present because they are part of God's covenant people ("I will make my covenant between me and you and your offspring, and I will be your God and you all will be my people"). Worship is the meeting of God's covenant people— all of them, regardless of age—with their Lord. When the covenant is renewed with the intergenerational assembly of Israel in Deuteronomy 29, Moses reminds them that they are "standing . . . before the LORD your God" (29:10), and that it is both with those present that God is making the covenant and "with whoever is not here with us today" (29:15). This latter statement is not just about the Israelites who skipped the meeting but refers to the intergenerational commitment that the Lord is a God to them and their offspring after them, for that day and for all time.

Peter picks up this passage in Acts 2 and intertwines it with another covenantal commitment from God in Isaiah 59:21:

> "As for me, this is my covenant with them," says the LORD:
> "My Spirit that is upon you, and my words that I have put
> in your mouth, shall not depart out of your mouth, or out
> of the mouth of your offspring, or out of the mouth of your
> children's offspring," says the LORD, "from this time forth
> and forevermore."

God's pledge is that he will grant his Spirit to his people and that this is an everlasting, intergenerational commitment. At Pentecost, Peter connects Deuteronomy 29 and

Isaiah in his answer to how people should respond to the gospel: "Repent and be baptized every one of you in the name of Jesus Christ for the forgiveness of your sins, and you will receive the gift of the Holy Spirit. For the promise is for you and for your children and for all who are far off, everyone whom the Lord our God calls to himself" (Acts 2:38–39). This response is a fusion of Deuteronomy 29:15 and Isaiah 59:21—God's covenant promise is for you and your children, and he will give his Spirit even to these.[7]

In other words, even in the New Testament, we see the continuity of the covenant community in its intergenerational character along with pledges from God to receive his Spirit by faith. How can we be before the presence of God? By his Spirit, who ensures that his Word will not leave us. Who is the recipient of this promise? All who believe, together with their children. What is worship? It is the people of God, bound by covenant, coming before their Father through the life of his Son by the power of his Spirit. Worship is God's people meeting with him.

After all, that is what the ordinary means of grace are: the means by which God meets us. The Holy Spirit uses word, water, and wine so that we might meet Jesus. And that goes for children as well as adults, for to such belong the kingdom of God.

When the disciples prevent parents from bringing children and infants to see Christ (Matt. 19:13–15; Mark 10:13–16; Luke 18:15–17), he is indignant (Mark 10:14). This is one of the few times Scripture expressly states that Jesus gets angry. That should give us immense pause. The kingdom of God belongs to God's children, and Jesus is outraged at the attempt to deny them access to him. We participate in God's kingdom in coming to Jesus and receiving him, which occurs through the ordinary means of grace. How do kids meet with Jesus? They worship alongside the rest of the family of God.

Following the triumphal entry and Christ cleansing the temple, Matthew records the priests and scribes in turn being indignant both at what Jesus did and at "the children crying out in the temple, 'Hosanna to the Son of David'" (Matt. 21:15). In the temple with Jesus, the children are before the Lord their God, offering up their praises. When challenged about the ruckus, Jesus responds by quoting Psalm 8:2: "Out of the mouth of infants and nursing babies you have prepared praise" (Matt. 21:16). God prepared praise for his Son in the cries of his littlest saints.

The church has a choice: We can be like the scribes, upset by the commotion of the children, or we can be like Jesus, who so welcomed and wanted the children to meet with him that disrupting their attendance was outrageous.

Common Obstacles and Objections to Including Kids in Worship

In the church I grew up in, pre-K children were in the service until the sermon, and then they were dismissed to a children's lesson in another part of the building. The first Sunday I was in kindergarten and able to stay in the service, my mom was serving in the nursery and my dad walked my younger brother to the children's lesson. While he was gone, I thought it would be funny to hide under the pew. When he got back and I was giggling, he told me to come out. My dad looked at me and said, "I'm not sure you're ready to be in here with us yet." I'm sure my dad has long forgotten that, but that comment immediately seared itself in my mind. I was ready, I did belong, and I was going to show it by how well I behaved.

When the expectations are high but achievable, kids meet the challenge. Sitting in worship is one such example. One of the reasons that kids in worship services can be so frustrating to parents and other adults is that they twitch and whisper and drop things. Kids can meet the high expectations of participation in the worship service, but parents need to remember that children are not being asked to be mini adults. They are still kids and are participating in the worship of God *as kids*.[8]

Pastors ensuring that children are welcome and encouraged to be in the worship of the church is the single most important way to put this into practice. However, even if we assent to the biblical picture, it can be bumpy when the rubber meets the road. Parents and churches may have different takes on the meaning of the biblical pattern or think it a nice ideal that has problems in implementation. To effectively incorporate children into the worship of the church with both parental and congregational buy-in requires addressing these practical hesitations.

The first common objection is that kids aren't actually learning anything in the service, especially during the sermon, since they're young and the content is aimed at adults. The line of reasoning is that in the same way we wouldn't put kindergartners in a ninth-grade class or mix toddlers with the youth group, it makes no sense to mix toddlers or young children with the adults on Sunday mornings. The kinds of objections in this camp run along these lines: The sermon and service will go over kids' heads, they won't be able to follow the sermon without it being dumbed down (although I've noticed that a good number of adults in my church seem more tuned in to the children's message than the sermon), and many of them can't read anyway, so the kids won't get anything out of it and will be bored.

Yet, by his Word and in worship, God speaks to his children.[9] Parents speak to, sing to, and smile at their kids when they're babies, and they do so regardless of whether the infants are able to pick up the specific meanings of their words. In fact, it is through this speaking to nonunderstanding children that kids learn how to speak back. Parents speak to kids with words the kids both know and don't know; that's the only way the kids learn new vocabulary in the first place. Moms and dads make noise that sounds like gibberish to babies but becomes intelligible words in their ears through exposure and familiarity. The same is true in worship, and just as the tone of a parent's coos communicates love and security to babies, the love and grace of God through his Word do the same to all his children.

God speaks to his kids regardless of their age. And this is the fundamental answer to the first objection: Worship is not a classroom but the covenant people of God meeting with their Father. It is a family gathering. The better comparison is not to the age and classroom gap between kindergarteners and high school students but to a family dinner. When the family gets together, the family eats and fellowships together. The point is the fellowship, even if learning also occurs. For instance, at the dinner table kids learn proper manners and how to conduct themselves as members of the family. They learn by *imitation*. The exact same is true in worship: Kids learn how to fear the Lord by imitating the rest of the family. That's what kids "get out of" worship. Including kids in worship is an example of authoritative parenting. When parents have high expectations for their kids ("You're joining us for worship, you're going to sit still during the sermon, and you're going to listen"), kids are invited to rise to the occasion and join in, like I as a kindergartner was by my dad.

That being said, kids learn far more doctrine and information from "adult" sermons and services than they are often given credit for. As all parents know, little ears are always listening, and we're constantly surprised by what they pick up and internalize. Churches shouldn't underestimate what kids grasp as they learn the rhythms of the gospel and the words of Scripture; kids are sponges, after all, and the amount they learn from a sermon is often surprising. Even when kids are "distracted" by coloring or snacks during a sermon, they hear and learn from God's Word. They're slowly being trained to do this even better. I've lost track of the number of times parents in my church have told me that their kids, who they thought were totally tuned out, asked them questions or talked to them about the sermon later. And this is exactly what we would expect from God's Word: The exposition of it is so even the littlest ones who don't know him may come to know and love and fear their Lord (Deut. 31:13).

The second common objection is that the subject matter in adult sermons is not age-appropriate. On the one hand, kids need to have age-specific teaching that meets them where they are, not simply a family gathering. Now, there is a time and place for age-focused discipleship like Sunday school, but including kids in corporate worship doesn't rule that out. On the other hand, there is the sense that children are not mature enough to engage with some biblical subject matter that should be addressed in sermons. A parent in my church once confronted me in anger after a service and invoked this as the reason. They pointed to the fact that I had preached "You shall not commit adultery" in a sermon, and they didn't think their kids (eight to ten years old) were ready to hear about such things and, moreover, shouldn't have to at their age.

Not every aspect of biblical teaching needs to be brought out in full detail in every sermon or teaching context. But in this case, the parent should have been encouraged to see that their kids needed to know the actual Bible. "You shall not commit adultery," one of the Ten Commandments, is certainly one of the doctrines parents are biblically expected to teach their children and was part of the law read during Israel's worship. When Paul delineated the fifth commandment in Ephesians 6:2–3, he expected the kids to know how it related to the other nine. The parent in this case was unwilling to have their kids read the Bible for fear of what they might stumble upon. Different topics could be used instead of the seventh commandment, but one of the functions of Scripture is to challenge what we think is acceptable and to prepare us for a life of following Jesus. The Bible knows us better than we know ourselves or our children.

Sensitive topics like adultery can be preached in a way that is PG. For instance, the First Catechism asks, "What does the seventh commandment teach you? To be pure in heart, language and conduct, and to be faithful in marriage." This is a biblically faithful and accurate way to speak about adultery, and a preacher can address the subject this way without lowering the bar for adults. At the same time, the First Catechism gives parents an approach to talk about these topics with their kids in follow-up conversations or when they are reading the Bible together without teaching kids that parts of the Bible or certain topics are off-limits to the full counsel of God.

One of the greatest obstacles churches encounter with incorporating kids in worship is the objection that the kids are a distraction to the other worshipers. Early on in our church's welcome of children in worship, there was a Sunday morning with a particularly fussy kid in our sanctuary's balcony. I was horrified to learn after the service that during the sermon, an older member of the church had walked up the stairs and glared at the family of the struggling kid. The poor parents were mortified and ashamed, and it took a lot of time and work to convince them to keep at it with their kids. They were afraid that their kids were unwanted, unwelcomed, and disruptive. On the other hand, for others in the congregation, it really was a struggle and distraction to have fussy kids present in the service.

Once again, overcoming this obstacle goes back to the point and purpose of worship: meeting with God. In this framework, kids are no more distracting from the purpose of worship than they were getting in the way of the adults when their parents brought them to Jesus. For older adults, the cultivation of patience and understanding of worship's purpose and the relationship of kids to it is absolutely necessary. This also is an opportunity for other adults to develop the virtues of attentive self-control, which they can use to help set examples for the kids, who watch how adults act.

After some time, the older adults in my church adjusted to and came to love having the children present. Hearing and seeing them in the services is still sometimes a distraction, just as having rambunctious kids at the dinner table can be, but they are still a joy. Fussy and wiggly kids in worship are not a failure but part of the family of God growing together.

For parents, this is often more difficult. Worship is intended to be a break from the tiresome routines of work and home, and when parents come into the service and still must be "on" because their kids are sitting with them, it can seem like stealing their Sabbath rest. Parents need to be fueled in order to fuel their kids, so if that spiritual rest is instead filled with watching over wiggly kids, then how can they fulfill their responsibility to their kids? Part of the answer is that bringing kids to worship is a component of this duty, so even in this work, parents are loving their kids. But additionally, this is why maintaining a spiritual life and fellowship (oxygen masks) are critical for parents. When Sunday worship can be mentally and physically draining and focusing on a fidgety kid keeps a parent from hearing all of the sermon, having additional areas for spiritual nourishment can be fueling.

A well-meaning congregant once complimented my wife, who sits alone during church with our kids since I'm preaching. They said that Lauren did a great job with our kids during the service, but that keeping the kids in line clearly meant worship was not a source of spiritual rest and refreshment and she needed a break. Lauren pointed out that the point of worship is not to be "refreshed," at least in that sense, and that spiritual rest occurs by resting upon Jesus as he is offered to us in the gospel, which is communicated to his people through the ordinary means of grace. When we go to church to physically and emotionally rest and be emotionally energized, we are distracted from the point of worship: to meet God and rest in him. Weary parents are refueled the same way any other worshiper is: through the gracious work of Christ's Holy Spirit.

How Churches Can Incorporate Children in Worship

So, in light of these obstacles, how can churches successfully incorporate children into their worship?

First, churches need to make it abundantly and enthusiastically clear that children of all ages are welcome and wanted in worship. The cries of infants and the fidgeting of toddlers are the sounds of God building his church. Pastors need to make clear to the congregation that these noises are not a distraction from corporate worship but part of it, even during the sermon. Pastors set the tone for a church's culture; the more pastors welcome and visibly value kids, the easier it will be for the congregation to do the same. Pastoral exhibitions of patience and love for even the kids who cry during their sermons teach not only the kids and parents that they're still welcome but the older adults what their posture toward kids should be.

Explicit and regular reminders that kids are welcome and wanted in worship go a long way toward establishing this. Our church's children's lesson occurs right before the sermon. The children of the church are invited to the front of the sanctuary, and whoever is preaching sits with them to lead the lesson, typically orbiting the First Catechism. This is a perfect setting to model talking with the kids and lets them know through how the pastor engages them that they are valued and loved. The kids are sent back to the pews following this lesson, but sometimes a kid will hang back for whatever reason to talk with the pastor. Exhibiting kindness and respect to them, rather than perfunctory dismissiveness, communicates to the kid that they are welcome and teaches the congregation how we should treat children.

Christianity is caught because it's taught, and it should be taught clearly in the worship service. The instinct is to dumb down the service or sermon to accommodate kids, but pastors should not talk down to the children. They are being invited into something meaningful and deep where they meet God, and they are expected to exercise their minds and spiritual muscles alongside their parents. Worship of God in the church is an act of faith. Worship and faith belong to children, and when these characterize their lives starting at the smallest age, they are theirs for life. Worship of God in the church is not something you graduate into once you mature but is the place where God forms the spiritual habits of even his littlest saints.

Yet there are ways to help accommodate children during the sermon even as they are incorporated. The simplest is to directly address them during the sermon: "Now, kids, this means . . ." Their ears prick up; they reengage and pay closer attention to what is being preached. Another way is explaining simple aspects of Scripture. I recently preached on John 1:29, where John the Baptist exclaims, "Behold, the Lamb of God, who takes away the sin of the world!" In my sermon I said, "Hey, kids, there are two Johns here, the John who wrote the book and John the Baptist. Now, kids, Jesus isn't literally a lamb, but John was saying he was just like a lamb. And what were lambs for in Jesus's day?"

The church can also do a lot to strengthen parents and grandparents with their kids in worship. Encouragement goes a long way for endurance, as does seeing the value of doing something hard like keeping squirmy kids in line during a sermon. From time to time I'll remind parents that we want them in the service with their kids, but if a kid is having trouble it's okay to step out with them to have them calm down and collect themselves. And if parents have to step out, we want them to feel the freedom to return without any embarrassment, so we tell them we want them and their child back with us.

There are a number of good books to help parents with their kids in the pews. Robbie Castleman's classic *Parenting in the Pew* is an excellent resource for parents, and I also recommend the illustrated children's book *God Made*

Me for Worship by Jared Kennedy for parents to help teach their kids. Every pew in our church has multiple copies of the card below, which has the dual purpose of encouraging the adults and giving the kids somewhere to draw.[10] We also have crayons and a coloring sheet with a picture connected to the sermon available to the kids.

A number of churches that welcome their kids in the worship service provide a series of five to seven discussion questions built around the sermon. These questions can double as a discussion guide for adult small groups and as a question a night over dinner between parents and their children to keep provoking thoughts on and attention to the sermon. A practice my wife adopted from the Dutch Reformed tradition is giving each of my kids a peppermint right before the sermon. This crumb-free treat is an incentive for good behavior and paying attention, the brisk kick from the mint keeps them focused and prevents them from dozing off during the sermon, and having something to suck on keeps them from talking. The traditional origin story of the candy cane has a similar motive: The candy cane was allegedly created to help kids keep quiet in church.[11] Peppermints are smaller than candy canes, but sometimes my preaching gets long-winded and it becomes a two-mint sermon. Having mints available is a small way to encourage kids and parents in the service.

Churches should also encourage older members of the church to be willing to sit with and assist younger families during the service (and younger parents to be willing to ask for help without embarrassment). This is a good way for those with experience, such as empty nesters and grandparents, to help out, and for those without kids to practice being part of the larger, intergenerational family of God. The development of friendships and relationships in the church

Children
at LPC

To parents of young children, may we suggest:

God gave vibrant energy that sometimes causes them to wiggle and make noise. They belong here with God's people where you have so faithfully brought them. Stick with it!

....

Parenting in church can be hard work but is a blessed part of our worship — our sacrificial offering to God.

....

Quietly explain the parts of the service, and the actions of the pastor, readers, and other congregants.

....

Sing the songs and participate in the prayers and responses. Children learn how to worship by watching you. ....

If you have to leave the service with your child, please feel free to do so, but please come back. As Jesus said, "Let the little children come to me."

To the members of our church:

Children are a gift. The sound of children in the church is the sound of Jesus keeping his promises; it is the sound of his church that lives on and never dies. Please welcome children and give a smile of encouragement to their parents.

PLEASE FEEL FREE TO LET YOUR CHILD USE THE BACK OF THIS CARD TO WRITE OR DRAW.

among the adults (oxygen masks!) is also necessary for this to work effectively. It is an especially invaluable practice for assisting single parents.

The biblical pictures and principles of incorporating children in worship are not rigid and provide wise guidelines. Being realistic as a congregation is necessary, as not only welcoming but also expecting kids in worship is not the norm for American churches and cuts across the grain of our culture. Most families coming to a church like this will not be used to it, and adjustments may take time.

Following the children's lesson in our services, parents have the choice to either have their kids rejoin them in the pew or send them to an age-focused lesson ("Covenant Kids") that runs the length of the sermon. We walk a tightrope here. We make absolutely and abundantly clear that we welcome and want our children in worship (and that's where my kids are; I regularly remind the church that if they want to know what I really believe, just see how I treat my kids), that we think this is a biblical practice, and that Covenant Kids is for families who aren't quite there. Part of the reason we stress children being welcome in worship is because the pressure on parents who want to keep their kids in the service will feel higher (due to their own fatigue, their kids who may want to leave, or a sense of expectation that if something is provided they need to utilize it), and we want to help relieve that. On the other hand, we don't want the families who do send their kids out to feel like second-class Christians, so we don't rub their faces in it.

What is done in this Covenant Kids lesson? There are several options, but since we treat it as provisional to tactfully help ease parents into incorporating their kids into worship, there are two paths we tend to follow. The first is to base the lesson on the sermon. I provide the teachers a short kid-oriented summary of the sermon (which also helps my regular sermon prep!), and they teach based on that so the kids and parents have the same topic to discuss. The other path is to make this time a worship training, explaining what worship is and preparing the kids for how to participate in it. The "Teach Me to Worship" curriculum from the Presbyterian Church in America is an excellent resource for this.[12]

The age cutoff is also a matter of wisdom. Some congregations might follow the biblical example of including everyone, even nursing babies, in the assembly of God. Others might use Nehemiah 8:2–3 as a guideline, encouraging kids to stay if they are developmentally able to process what they hear. This is a good principle: Are kids developmentally able to process what they're hearing, even if at a rudimentary and incomplete level? If so, they should be included in worship. Determining the specific age range for this requires wisdom on a congregation-by-congregation basis.

Finally, it's good to remember that kids have something to teach the church. Jesus uses the faith of children as an example for the church to emulate (Matt. 18:3–4), and their presence in the service to do just that should never be discounted. Our church recites the Lord's Prayer together every Sunday, and there is nothing quite as wonderful as hearing that slightly higher, slightly off-time voice of a child giving it their all as they pray as Jesus instructed. The voice of a child praying to their heavenly Father demonstrates to his church sincere and true faith, and God has prepared for himself praise out of the mouths of babes.

Chapter 5

MORE THAN PROGRAMS
Kids Need the Whole Family of God

When it comes to passing down the faith to the next generation, programs like Sunday school or youth group, while helpful, are less effective than simply sharing life together as a church.

A high school student in my church once approached me because she wanted to invest more deeply in the church and grow in her faith. She had recently participated in a youth mission trip and, like so many other teenagers, found the singular focus on serving Jesus exhilarating. She had been lukewarm in her faith up to that point and didn't want to lose this new spiritual fervor. She realized her old patterns hadn't produced that kind of spiritual intensity and she hadn't been properly investing in the ordinary rhythms of the Christian life. She wanted desperately to keep growing in her faith in the normal seasons of life. There was just one problem: Her parents were completely uninterested in anything more than superficial religiosity.

That's why she was coming to me for advice. She very much wanted to be at church regularly and to have a home where prayer, Bible reading, and conversations about Jesus were normal. But she felt unsupported in her Christian walk by her parents, who were members of our church.

Every pastor has had some version of this experience. On the one hand, it's exciting, because a young woman benefited from the ministry of the church and wants to keep growing in her faith. That's the dream! On the other hand, it's deeply frustrating, because her parents are disengaged and passive in the Christian nurture of their daughter. Any efforts by the church to disciple this student will be like trying to swim upstream, with little to no support from the most influential people in her life, and their passivity silently instructs her that a more invested faith is unnecessary.

We know faith is most effectively passed on through parents. So how can the church ground kids in the faith when their parents just don't care or aren't available?

Adamczyk and Smith found that kids who regularly participate in a faith community that interacts with and supports one another throughout the week were more likely to keep their faith into adulthood.[1] Following parental influence and incorporation into worship, regular participation in the religious community is the third meaningful characteristic of children who hold on to their faith, and this is true both for kids whose parents are already invested in their faith and for kids whose parents are not. What is especially valuable is not peer-to-peer relationships but when spiritually mature adults in the church are engaged with, know, and care about the kids in their community.

The church is not merely a collection of individuals or programs—it is the family of God, a communion of saints across generations. When children are meaningfully incorporated into the full life of this intergenerational family beyond just Sunday worship (see the previous chapter), and when they are known, loved, and mentored by spiritually mature adults in the church, their faith is far more likely to endure. Moral formation and faith retention happen in the context of real community, where belonging is prioritized over structured programs. Programs like Sunday school and youth group are not a substitute for true spiritual relationships and can even undermine faith retention if they unintentionally separate children from the broader church family. Pastors and church leaders must recognize this reality and intentionally shape the church's culture and resources to foster deep, lasting connections within the family of God.

The Church Is the Family of God

The most important biblical metaphor for the church is family. Examples of this description abound in Scripture, especially the New Testament. Perhaps the best description of this comes from Jesus in Mark 10:17–31. A rich man asks Jesus what he needs to do to inherit eternal life. Jesus tells him to sell all he has and give the proceeds to the poor. The man leaves, upset because he has many valuable possessions.

Jesus explains that the problem is the man loved his money and resources and couldn't see past the cost of their sacrifice to the greater good of the kingdom of God. Peter points out to Jesus the difference between the rich man and the disciples: The disciples in fact had left everything to follow Jesus. Peter is not trying to justify the disciples or put them on a pedestal but is making a rhetorical point: "Jesus, you told this rich guy to give up all his money to find the kingdom of God. We did just that—but we don't seem to have gained anything yet."

Jesus responds, "Truly, I say to you, there is no one who has left house or brothers or sisters or mother or father or children or lands, for my sake and for the gospel, who will not receive a hundredfold now in this time, houses and brothers and sisters and mothers and children and lands, with persecutions, and in the age to come eternal life" (vv. 29–30).

Christ's answer to Peter is that anyone who comes after Jesus will have to sacrifice things they love. For some people, like the rich man, that's possessions and money. For others, like Peter and the disciples, it's home and family. The disciples don't seem to have been cut off from their loved ones by following Jesus but had left them behind for significant periods of time to be on the road with him. Yet there will be those whose families will reject them because of their faith in Christ.

What does Jesus say those people will gain in return? A home and a family—not just any home and family but one superabundant compared to what they lost. And this isn't something we need to wait for in the age of eternal life; it begins "now in this time."

Jesus is speaking about the church. Those who follow after him have been admitted into the family of God. In that family are all the others who have been joined to Christ—parents and siblings and children—and the numbers in the family of God are far greater than what we have naturally.

Jesus is telling Peter that, yes, the disciples have sacrificed much to follow him, but they have also gained much more than they realized. They have gained a family, the church of Christ, which is the household of God's kingdom.

The church as God's family is called to behave as a family. This is especially important to remember when people who are without their own natural family or whose natural family is unsupportive of their Christian walk come through our doors. When Jesus speaks of gaining homes and families, he means that the church will act as a family by caring for its members. The church is God's surrogate family for those who are without their own. And for the church to act like a family means that we are to live life together as a family, with the kind of regular routines and relationships that characterize healthy natural families.

When the church behaves like a family, children gain parents in the faith a hundredfold, and their faith is cultivated and strengthened. This is a great gospel hope for kids whose parents aren't invested and for single parents who feel like they're alone. And it's a call to action for the church.

The Communion of Saints Is Intergenerational

An older couple attended our church faithfully for decades, until the wife's dementia made it impossible. Her decline was rapid and her death sudden. After her death, her husband returned to church and sat in their old pew. In the brief interim between her decline and his return, my family had begun sitting in that row. That Sunday morning when the husband came back alone, he sat down next to my five-year-old son. Matthias had missed seeing them, and when he sat down, Matthias scooted closer, leaned against his shoulder, grabbed his hand, and told him he was glad to be sitting next to him.

Standing at the pulpit, all I could see were the tears on his cheeks.

Our church has a fellowship hour after each worship service, a time to socialize over snacks and coffee. We have a wonderful space to do this, with lots of tables for people to settle in. A group of older members of the church—some in their nineties down to some in their sixties—usually sits together to catch up and enjoy each other's company. I typically make the rounds, visiting with all the different tables and groups of people. One Sunday I came over to sit with the older crowd and started to plop into the only open seat. Cindy, one of those at the table, started to tell me that seat was saved, when I heard a loud, indignant protest: "Dad! That's *my* seat!" Matthias had claimed the spot as his own for that Sunday, much to the amusement of the elders.

However, it was not to be a one-off. Every week from then on out, Matthias has picked his go-to spot at the table with the older members of the church. Now, it's not because he's trying to be a Boy Scout or something; he probably suspects his mother is not as hawkeyed with him there, and the grandparental demeanor of the table allows for extra desserts. But he sits with them because they are his people now. His spot, self-determined, is with the elders of the church, regardless of how much dessert his mother limits him to. And it's not just that Matthias is a creature of habit (his younger sister less consistently joins him); he actually likes the people at the older table, and they like him. Their care for and interest in him is reciprocated like in any relationship or friendship.

Sociologist Jean Twenge in her groundbreaking 2023 work *Generations* documents how younger generations are less and less connected to their older-generation cohorts.[2] The disappearance of shared third spaces—the areas of life where people gather outside their home for community and socialization—has meant that with the exception of immediate family, most kids do not interact with older adults. The church is one of the last bastions of this cross-generational interaction.

Casual and valuable intergenerational interactions, like with Matthias in the pew or in the fellowship hall, are vanishingly rare in the rest of the country. Outside of schools or youth sports, where the relationship between adults and children is formalized by schedules, divided by grade and class, and limited by year, there are few areas where unrelated kids and adults interact, and even the few counterexamples are typically between a group of kids and one or two individual adults, not a community that includes a vast array of kids and adults in differing life stages.

I officiate a number of funerals every year, including some for people not part of our church community. When the funeral is for a member of the church, kids are in attendance. What has struck me at funerals for nonchurched or dechurched people is that outside of their immediate family, kids do not attend funerals for older adults (i.e., those who die of natural causes) because they don't know any. The data, like Twenge's work, reveals that kids on the whole increasingly don't know older adults who aren't family or teachers, and this manifests in funeral attendance. This is a historical aberration and a snapshot of how our country has become increasingly generationally siloed and socially estranged. The church is one of the last communities where children can organically interact with older adults and come to know them well enough to mourn their death in a funeral.

Yet, while the church confesses that we believe in the "communion of saints," that has practically become a belief in the communion of our peers rather than the fuller family of God. The church has by and large embraced a discipleship strategy of age segregation, having kids spend as much time as possible around their peers in age-specific classes or groups as the primary vehicle of discipleship. Yes, adults are present in the role of teachers or small group facilitators (a good thing), but intergenerational cross-pollination is limited.

The value of these missed relationships in social benefits is significant. Social psychologist Matthew Lieberman has established that the benefit to our well-being from different kinds of relationships, including regular interactions with neighbors, ranges from the equivalent of $60,000 to $100,000 in additional income.[3] For kids, this is not limited to interactions with peers, parents, family, or teachers but includes being embedded in an intergenerational community. We are built for the communion of saints, and our kids benefit greatly from social participation in such a fellowship.

Together these observations may amount to a series of interesting thoughts and pleasant aspirations for the way kids and adults in the church might know one another, and that is all they would amount to if left alone. But the more kids know and are known by the adults in their church community, the more likely they are to retain their Christian faith.

Moral Formation and Faith Retention Happen in Community

The most effective church programs for handing down the faith are not programs at all but simply sharing life together as God's family. Children learn by observing, imitating, and participating in the life of the community. The laughter, conversations, and shared meals of the church family provide a tangible experience of what it means to belong to God's people, and the people become *their people* and the church becomes *their church*, not just their youth group. The community of the church is an extended family network that can amplify parents' investment in their kids. That amplification can range in strength, but a thick church community makes it easier for kids without supportive parents to have an extended network of faith support.

Richard Weaver, a mid-twentieth-century scholar and intellectual historian, put it this way in his posthumous classic *Visions of Order*:

> The difference [between instruction and education] is an important one, since education means not merely the impartation of information to the mind but the shaping of the mind and of the personality. Instruction may be limited to the transmission of facts and principles it is desirable to know as a body of knowledge, but education is unavoidably a training for a way of life. Education comprises instruction, of course, but it goes beyond instruction to a point that makes it intimately related to the preservation of a culture.[4]

Education in the Christian faith is the shaping of the soul through the culture of God's people, which includes its worship and community. Through the way it shares life together, the church shapes the mind and soul of its children, and when it becomes intergenerationally stratified, it fails in "the preservation of [its] culture"—it fails to pass down the faith in a life-long discipleship. A thick community of the saints forms and educates the kids of the church into lifelong disciples of Jesus.

Adamczyk and Smith argue along similar lines that a distinguishing feature between families whose kids hold on to the faith and those whose kids don't is whether they treat religion as a "community solidarity project" versus a "personal identity accessory."[5] In a community solidarity project, faith is not just an individual pursuit but a shared journey, where the religious congregation serves as the center of local faith life. Spiritual growth happens through active participation in the community, shaping individuals toward the true good. In contrast, a personal identity accessory approach treats religion as a tool for coping with life, where congregations exist primarily to provide supportive resources, and growth is seen as a matter of personal reflection.[6]

The children who retained their faith into adulthood were deeply embedded in a religious community that served as the anchor of their spiritual and social lives—both they and their families participated in something greater than themselves. Conversely, those who left the church came from families who treated faith as an accessory to their self-identity— easily discarded when it no longer felt useful. Lifelong faith was far more likely when both children and their families were truly incorporated into the life of the community.

What characterized communities of faith that were effective in handing off the faith to kids were godly, committed adults invested in addition to the children's parents. When kids see that other adults deeply care about and have their regular lives shaped by their faith, then the community becomes an effective channel for the parents in the church and an effective community for kids whose parents are absent.

For this reason, churches should prioritize creating spaces and opportunities where adults and children can engage with one another outside of formal programs. Hosting children in homes, involving them in everyday activities around the church, and simply enjoying time with them can profoundly impact their faith. These informal interactions show children that they are seen, valued, and loved by the broader church family. They also reinforce the truth that being part of the body of Christ is about belonging, not performance or mere knowledge.

To cultivate this kind of intergenerational community, churches should encourage adults and parents to intentionally know and invest in the children of the church. This means actively engaging with kids during fellowship hours, greeting them warmly, and taking an interest in their lives. It also means opening up homes and inviting children and teens into everyday spaces. Whether it's for a meal, a game night, or simply time spent together, these interactions can be transformative. For teenagers in particular, this structure is invaluable for reinforcing buy-in to the faith and church; youth events in people's homes strengthen these bonds and culture and make the development of relational hubs between families within the church more natural. It also means that the church should make the effort to incorporate kids into the times of "adult" fellowship such as men's and women's events. While there is value in and a time and place for kids-free adult fellowship (the oxygen mask—and as a parent of three young kids, I say yes, please!), making the effort to integrate the kids into the programs of the whole community, not just age-siloed events, is a practical and straightforward way to implement intergenerational community. It also allows for older and single adults to get to know the kids of the church within the context of church life.

"Does My Son Know You?"

In 2022, The Ringer's NBA staff writer Jonathan Tjarks published an unusual piece for the sports site. Tjark had been diagnosed with a rare form of cancer and was reflecting on what had changed in his life and the likelihood of his own death. Sadly, he died six months after the essay's publication. What was arresting in his essay was his recounting of becoming part of a life group at his church and the charge he had given them as he faced death. At a young age, Tjarks had lost his own father to a prolonged fight with Parkinson's, and he said, "There were a bunch of people at his funeral whom I hadn't seen in years. They all told me how sorry they were and asked whether there was anything they could do. All I could think was I don't know any of you. I know *of* you. I've heard your names. But I don't *know* you."[7]

Tjarks had his own young son, and he told the members of his life group, "When I see you in heaven, there's only one thing I'm going to ask—Were you good to my son and my wife? Were you there for them? Does my son *know* you? . . . I want him to wonder why his dad's friends always come over and shoot hoops with him. Why they always invite him to their houses. Why there are so many of them at his games. I hope that he gets sick of them."[8]

Tjarks's desire for his son is one that should resonate with every loving parent, and yet far too often in the life of the church it is not something that actually occurs. Whether a child is orphaned or abandoned by a parent, too often they are not known by the men and women of the church.

The resonance of Tjarks's hope lies in what we intuitively grasp: Kids need good adult role models, ones who don't observe at a distance but are invested interpersonally with the child. When a parent is tragically absent, the risk of not having that kind of invested model surges.

We want our kids to be known and loved. Tjarks was not merely hoping that friends in his life group would begin knowing his son once he died; he actively worked for them and his son to know each other before that point. He spoke about how the first step in this process was to personally invest in and become integrated into the life group (putting on his own oxygen mask) in order to be known himself, to establish the genuine friendships. Tjarks needed to be in community first.

Now, this is not always how things play out in the church. Almost by definition the parents who are least likely to care for their kids are the least likely to invest in a godly community. And this is where the church's duty to intentionally and diligently act as a family—and ensure that the kids of the church are known in intergenerational and interpersonal relationships—comes in.

At its heart, the mission and purpose of the church are deeply familial. This is what Jesus teaches in Mark 10:28–31, and it permeates all aspects of the church's life. For instance, the dynamics of a loving family gathered together in joy mirror the gathering of the church in worship, united by their shared union with Christ. The people of God are adopted into the family of God with him as our Father and Jesus as our elder brother.[9] In worship the church is like the prodigal son returning—but in joyful faith—to the prepared feast of our Father. Baptism is the admission into this community, and typically the administration of this sacrament is accompanied by commitments from the congregation. This is particularly true in churches that baptize infants but is true for all churches regardless of the age of the recipient. Some churches have these commitments expressed by godparents, godly individuals who can vouch for the faith of the parents or the baptized and who pledge to assist in their growth in faith. Others, like my own Presbyterian congregation, stress that it is the whole congregation that makes this commitment.

In my church's service of baptism, the congregation vows to take responsibility for the child's continued Christian nurture, to set a godly example for them, to pray for them, to assist the child's parents in their own spiritual health, and to provide all they can to help in the child growing up to profess faith in Jesus. Leaving aside the debates over infant versus believer's baptism, most churches expect their congregations to make similar commitments to whoever receives the sacrament of baptism. These are promises to welcome the baptized into the family and treat them as a member. The older adults are committing to become spiritual surrogate parents to the child, and the baptized are welcomed in as brothers and sisters. The sacrament of baptism is a commitment to be the family Jesus promised in Mark 10:28–31.

A concrete picture of this is in the Lord's Supper, the covenant, family meal of God's people. This sacrament is a divinely ordained expression of the unity of God's people with him through his Son, and it symbolizes the shared life believers have in Christ. The Eucharist is God the Father's children gathered together in a dinner served by his Son through the power of the Holy Spirit. Worship is a family get-together with a family meal. The fellowship (communion) of the saints is centered on the table and extends outward.

This familial dynamic and mission is not confined to the church building or the worship service. It emanates from our union with Christ expressed in shared worship and extends into everyday life, as Christians live together before the face of God. Fellowship among the saints—regular, intentional time spent together—is a core practice of the Christian faith because that is how we live as God's family. And it is a core practice because through this participation the members of God's family grow in their commitment to the family and to their God.

Incorporating kids into this family-fellowship dynamic is crucial. This is not something that can be programmed and requires the intentional cultivation of a fellowship ecosystem. It's the difference between having an age-segregated Sunday school program and having an intergenerational fellowship hour. While the former can be organized and scheduled, the latter requires a different kind of effort.

Like with corporate worship, kids need to be incorporated into the fellowship of the church, the whole church. Integration into the regular rhythm of the congregation's life, including and beyond worship, is the key for children to know and be known by others in the life of the church. The more a child's life of faith is a natural extension of their day-to-day life and finds expression in participation with the intergenerational community of the church, the stronger their faith will grow. When the whole family of faith becomes their family, their faith is not just their parents' but becomes their own. In short, when it comes to faith retention and growth, fellowship hours are more effective than Sunday school or youth group. Kids know and are known by not just their teachers and peers but the family of God.

The people of the church spending time together is foundational for forming a robust and lasting community of faith. This is especially critical for children and teenagers, who are in a formative stage of life where relationships and experiences shape their understanding of God, faith, and the church. One of the most impactful ways the church can nurture the faith of its young members is by encouraging faithful parents and adults to actively host and invest in the children of the congregation. When adults in the church open their homes and spend intentional time with children and teens, they create opportunities for mentorship, discipleship, and genuine connection. This is particularly transformative for children from homes where faith is not actively practiced or where parental involvement is lacking. In these cases, the presence of spiritual surrogate parents—adults who model Christlike love and attentiveness—can fill a vital gap. These relationships communicate to children that they are part of a larger family in Christ and are loved and valued. They also demonstrate that the faith is not merely a set of teachings but a way of life rooted in fellowship, from Christ to us and through Christ by his Spirit to each other. As churches consider how to disciple the next generation, fostering these intergenerational bonds is one of the most effective ways to ensure children are connected to the larger body of Christ and will grow in their faith.

As I was growing up, a family in my church hosted a Sunday evening Bible study in their home. Multiple families with kids ranging from toddlers to college age joined together, along with singles, single parents, and empty nesters. The high school and back-home college students often brought their friends. The study began with everyone together in the living room watching a sermon together,[10] and then the kids went into another room to discuss the sermon under the guidance of the older teens while the adults stayed behind to have their discussion. After a while the kids returned and there was a general, adult-guided discussion. What I recall most is not the quality of the discussion or the educational effectiveness of the study format but how natural the whole thing was. Hosts Gary and Patti often had the teenagers of the church over; the families all got together often; and the kids of the church were known by the adults, who cared deeply about their faith and about them as people. This worked because there was an ecosystem of relationships, care, and faith that made a study like this a natural extension of faith life.

Without the investment and efforts of adults and parents to forge these relationships and create settings where this kind of study could happen (oxygen masks!), it would never have occurred. This extended church network was not a replacement for my own parents—not by a long shot—but it did supplement and support them. It was a practical, loving, organic outworking of the baptismal vow of the congregation to assist in the spiritual nurture of kids and to support parents in that work. For those kids (especially teenagers) who were interested in deepening their faith in Christ without real parental encouragement, this established a setting to foster that faith and provide a space for spiritual surrogate parents to mentor them in their faith.

One of the simplest and most powerful ways to embody these kinds of relationships is through the sharing of meals and time. This is the natural emanation of Eucharistic fellowship to the regular lives of the ordinary Christian. When members of the church gather around a table, engage in conversation, and share their lives with one another, they practice the kind of familial love that Christ established. Such practices teach all members, young and old, that faith is lived in community, not isolation.

When I was a teenager, a (different!) family in my church regularly had the youth over at their house. They had several teenagers themselves, and their house became a kind of social hub. But more than that, their home became a place where we were able to be comfortable and talk about life, be heard, and receive godly wisdom. It was natural for us to show up, get served pancakes, and have conversations about faith and life. The integration of regular life, church family, and faith meant that personal faith in Jesus was not compartmentalized but rather that Christian living was a shared commitment and burden.

This communal integration works in the organic relationships in churches through the intentional incorporation of kids in the "adult" fellowship events. The men in my church hold a monthly Saturday morning breakfast with a speaker, which is predominantly patronized by the older members of the congregation. I started bringing Matthias when he was five, and it wasn't always easy to get a sleepy little boy up at 7:00 a.m. on a Saturday! For the longest time, the other men assumed that this was typical pastor behavior—the minister dragging his kids to all the church stuff against their will. But the truth is much better: Matthias loved it, even when he was the only kid there at first. Kids love what their parents love and get excited for what their parents are excited for, and Matthias loved that he had something to do with Dad. And not just with Dad but with the *men*. He was being welcomed into the activities of men as one of us.

When Matthias learns on Monday that there is a men's breakfast that weekend, it's all he can talk about that week. And this isn't just a boy thing. The women in my church have similar events, and their daughters have a similar response. Another church I served had bimonthly speakers at men's dinners, often barbecue, and the teen guys always showed up in droves. They usually stayed at their own table, but they were together with and known by the fathers of the church.

From Participation to Graduation: When Programs Replace Belonging

This approach to integrating kids into the life of the faith community protects against one of the great dangers of privileging age-segregated approaches to discipleship: kids growing up and out of church. Adamczyk and Smith noted that things like Sunday school, youth group, and confirmation could actually be counterproductive and dangerous to the faith retention of kids whose parents sent them to church but were only loosely committed to Christianity themselves.[11] How so? By teaching kids that faith and religious commitment are part of childhood and things from which they could graduate. In the same way that driver's ed classes are no longer needed once student drivers get their license, these kinds of programs can teach kids that faith and the church may be preparation for adulthood, but upon successful graduation into real life, they can be left behind like any other accessory. It is only when these programs are intertwined as channels with parental influence for forming solidarity with the community of the church that they are helpful to faith retention, rather than inadvertently undermining it.

This is not an either-or proposition, where churches must choose between a tightly knit intergenerational community on the one hand and Sunday school and youth group on the other. But the former is more effective for faith retention than the latter, so at the very least this should inform how local churches allocate their resources and design their programming. More critical than getting a good youth program up and running is the church acting intentionally so we can answer a dying father's question, "Does my son know you?" in the affirmative. Most churches would probably heartily agree with this, yet how we staff our congregations, spend our money, and organize our volunteers does not communicate that agreement.

The challenges to aligning the church's resources with these principles emerge in three different ways, and while these will manifest differently in each congregation, it is helpful to identify them in order to be better prepared in navigating them. First, it is far more difficult to plan and organize a culture than a classroom. Getting youth volunteers is difficult enough; developing a church culture where a formal, organized youth group is unnecessary because of how parents and families of the church spend time together is far harder. Compared to making your house a hub for church youth, volunteering one to two hours a week to serve in children's ministry is an easy sacrifice. Pastors can teach on this topic week in and week out, but unless the people of the church put it into practice, it just seems like an impossible ideal. And then when someone is willing to volunteer their time to lead a class or teen small group and nothing else is happening, of course the church jumps on the opportunity.

The second challenge is nostalgia and shame. Parents who had a good experience in their own youth group, who have fond memories of Sunday school, whose kids really enjoyed their youth experience, or whose church has always had confirmation simply won't believe there is a better way. Suggesting that things be done differently by deprioritizing the traditional approaches, which have been supported and taught by godly men and women, feels like shaming them and denigrating their years of service, the data notwithstanding. The old saying often attributed to Mark Twain, "It's easier to fool people than to convince them that they have been fooled," could be rephrased as "It's easier to keep doing what we've been doing and love doing than to convince us that there is a better way." The perennial retort that "It worked for me and my kids, so why should we be different now?" makes any change difficult. And this is dialed up to a ten whenever kids are involved.

And that's because, third, America is a matrilineal society. Matrilineal societies are "centuries old systems that organize community life so that the day-to-day activities of women are placed at the center of social thriving for successive generations."[12] This is not a criticism of American society or women but an acknowledgment of the social dynamics at play in churches. In a matrilineal society, the daily family operations are handled by women, and institutions that have contact with children (e.g., schools, churches) are successful insofar as they support women and are supported by them. Professor and author Anthony Bradley explains how this has affected American evangelicalism:

> Women in matrilineal societies would enlist the help of platonically connected men, often brothers, uncles, and grandfathers, to have an impact on children's lives. In suburban churches, that role was professionalized in the office of "youth pastor" or "pastor of youth and families," and so on. It should come as no surprise that the children's and youth ministry roles emerged as central to evangelical churches because of the economic and geographical nature of the nuclear family in a matrilineal America. It is not true, as it is often intimated, that youth ministry exists to "assist" the family or to reach the children. Many believe themselves to be doing that as a justification for their existence.
>
> But in today's matrilineal America, especially in the suburbs, children's ministry, youth ministry, family ministry, and other post–World War II church staff titles specifically exist to serve and assist mothers in passing down the essentials of faith. Ask any children's or youth ministry staff what would happen if all of the mothers pulled out of helping them run their ministries versus the fathers. Children's ministry and

youth ministry exist because communities and churches are primarily matrilineal.[13]

Why does this make deprioritizing youth group and Sunday school more difficult? Because stressing an approach to discipling children that prioritizes the whole community and parents—mothers *and* fathers—involves removing a piece of support for women, the very people who tend to drive children to church. A community-centered approach to child discipleship requires fathers to be actively invested, which cuts across the grain of a matrilineal society and most moms' expectations and credulity. Similarly, even for the women who volunteer several hours a week with kids and teens, replacing that model with something that requires opening up a home or hosting can feel like swapping something that supports them for an energy-draining "support." Being a kids' ministry teacher is also less interpersonally costly than participating in an intergenerational Bible study.

Again, the prioritization of a community-centered approach to childhood discipleship does not preclude programs like Sunday school or youth group. But the tendency, which requires pastoral grit to resist, is to say, "Yeah, yeah, we want the whole church involved," and then focus on programs. Programs can be helpful, but the horse needs to come before the cart: The quality of programs needs to be assessed in light of whether they support or undercut the church knowing its kids and the kids being invested in the church. Kids knowing and being known by others in the regular community life of the church are indispensable for forging lifelong discipleship.

Chapter 6

KEEPING THE HORSE BEFORE THE CART
Programs Reinforce Parental Influence

For many American Christians, "childhood discipleship" is synonymous with "Sunday school." Yet, in the history of the global church, Sunday school is relatively new. In *Parents and Children*, published in 1897, Charlotte Mason bemoaned the advent and widespread adoption of Sunday school, not because it was new but because it was a "necessary evil."[1] Parents in Britain had neglected their "first duty"—instructing their children in the faith—and needed a substitute to step into that role. Children were to be educated in the faith at home and then come to church to worship alongside their parents. When parental catechesis declined, rather than letting the spiritual education of children slide, the church decided training kids in the details and doctrine of the faith was a necessity. The church's widespread embrace of the

Sunday school model, with its corresponding decline in faith transmission, was the evil Mason lamented.

Mason observed more than a century ago what sociologists have confirmed over and over again: Church programs are no substitute for parental investment in kids for childhood faith retention. And yet the church overwhelmingly invests its time and money in Sunday school or equivalent age-segregated, peer-to-peer-focused discipleship models. This phenomenon is driven partially by concerns about parents neglecting their first duty, but mostly—if it's even given conscious consideration—it's driven by the belief that inculcating Christianity is the church's duty. Still, churches recognize that parental investment is necessary and invaluable, even when the church takes on the responsibility of kids' ministry and programming. So why is it so difficult for churches to pivot their strategy?

The church often places the cart of programming before the horse of parental investment in the discipleship of children, unintentionally obscuring the more crucial role parents play in passing along the faith. Churches frequently allocate their resources toward these programs rather than prioritizing the cultivation of a familial culture, so that things like Sunday school and youth group are servants of the greater objective of faith retention and lifelong discipleship. When the order is reversed—when programming functionally leads rather than supports—the result is misplaced prioritization that weakens the very impact these ministries are meant to have. This misalignment is understandable, as keeping the horse and cart properly arranged is no simple task. To do so, we must examine first why this challenge persists and then how church programming can be structured to reinforce, rather than replace, the essential role of parental influence.

The *Real* Value in Children's Programming

In addition to the previously discussed American matrilineal culture, the answer to why it is so difficult to move away from a largely program-based ministry is the bad optics of "cutting" VBS, youth group, or Sunday school. This is invariably seen as the church abandoning its commitment to children rather than adjusting for improvement. This is especially true of smaller churches feeling market pressure from their larger neighbors.[2] When parents seek out churches, "strong" children's and youth programming (i.e., large numbers of kids and activities) is far more appealing than a church that promotes aprogrammatic discipleship. To parents looking for a community for their kids, lack of formal programming looks like the church doing nothing for children. They worry their kids won't have friends. This sense of competition incentivizes churches to maintain their programming.[3]

Some of this difficulty is also due to programmatic inertia. It's a lot easier to replicate what is currently in place (or what parents and volunteers remember doing as kids) than to scrap that and do something different. Trying to swap out any beloved programs meets resistance, and doubly so when kids are involved. And when parents and volunteers have fond memories and feel that the current approach is working, asking them to embrace a different way that they've never seen and has little structure is asking them for a leap of faith. Statistics are rarely persuasive against people's lived experience and ingrained habits.

But the main difficulty is that children's ministry programs do have some value. It's not a zero-sum game, which is why Mason denounced *parents* using Sunday school to shirk their first duty, not churches trying to stand in the gap. Even when parents are doing their job raising their kids, children's ministry can be beneficial to handing down the faith. The problem is that the cart of programming is too easily placed before the horse of parental investment, and this far more crucial dimension of passing along the faith is obscured with the church's investment in the programming. To see how the church can keep the horse and cart properly ordered, we need to understand how children's ministry programming can be valuable in the first place.

The first value is channeling. Parents who are committed to the faith of their kids use classes as channels to invest in and build up their children's faith.[4] We saw channeling used with the incorporation of kids in the worship and community of the church, and it applies to programming as well. Channeling is when parents intentionally arrange for religious formation of their children outside of the regular, routine relationship and interactions between them. Channeling involves guiding children into activities and relationships that reinforce rather than replace the direct influence of the parents. Effective channeling subtly introduces and steers children toward positive religious experiences (authoritative parenting). It is intentional and strategic without being controlling or oppressive, focusing on creating opportunities, fostering connections, and encouraging participation without resorting to coercion, bribery, or begging. The purpose of religious channeling is to help children gradually personalize and internalize their faith and identity. When done effectively, channeling enables children to grow into individuals who actively believe and practice their own faith rather than simply following their parents' lead (the authoritarian model). Channeling involves arranging various influences in the kids' lives that support this transition, fostering an environment where faith becomes their own.

The most effective form of channeling is the connection and engagement between kids and the nonfamily adults embedded in the religious community. This is where children's ministry programming becomes valuable: when it functions effectively as a channel for parents to warmly push their kids toward religious engagements. To be clear, the value of these classes is downstream of and effective because of parents who are already committed to their kids' faith. Channeling works as a reinforcement of, not a replacement for, a parent's first duty.

The second value of children's ministry programming is why Mason thought Sunday school was lamentably necessary in the first place: Parents don't always teach their kids the Christian faith, and this is obviously true when they aren't Christians themselves. Children's ministries and church programs can play a pivotal role in engaging families and fostering faith, particularly among increased secularization that means many (Christian!) parents don't know their faith. In many cases, these children are not actively involved in worship services or integrated into the broader life of the church, and their parents won't try to rectify that but will send them to VBS or youth group. This gap means children's ministries can act as critical bridges, serving as an accessible entry point for kids and families loosely connected to the church.

Furthermore, children's ministries can serve as valuable on-ramps for faith exploration. Like missionary outposts, these programs create initial contact points where children who are otherwise disconnected from Christianity can encounter the gospel and Christ's church.

In this case, the value of these ministries lies in their potential to connect children and families to the broader, more enduring practices of faith transmission. While a class or youth group alone may not be sufficient to instill lasting faith, these touchpoints can guide families toward greater involvement in worship, discipleship, and community life. In this sense, children's ministries are not really programs for discipling the kids of Christian parents but are forms of outreach to a non-Christian world, where kids can experience the community of Christ's family. This is a different objective of children's ministry, even if it is compatible with parental channeling. Being conscious of these distinct goals is indispensable when it comes to organizing children's programs so as not to lose sight of the objective of handing down the faith.

Channeling and missionary outposts are the chief benefits of children's ministry, but for them to work effectively toward those benefits, the horse and cart must be properly ordered. How churches implement these programs can reverse the horse-cart arrangement and undermine passing along the faith.

Pastoral Messaging on Children's Ministry Prioritization

The first and most crucial way to ensure that programs exist to reinforce rather than replace parental influence happens on a practical level through consistent teaching and pastoral leadership. Because of the vital role they play in shaping the culture and priorities of their congregations, pastors must take the lead in setting the tone on children's discipleship. A significant aspect of this responsibility is effective communication, ensuring that the principles for keeping kids

Christian are embraced by staff, elders, parents, and volunteers. Most pastors have experienced sharing strategy and biblical truth in meetings and sermons, witnessing the appearance of their acceptance, then running smack-dab into the wall of existing habits and culture. If the horse and cart of parental channeling are to be properly arranged, pastors need to persistently, patiently, firmly, and gently teach their congregations.

Pastors need to explicitly convey that the value of children's ministries and youth groups lies in their ability to reinforce parental influence, not replace it. In the same way that routine conversations about faith should characterize how parents interact with their children, the nature of parental influence and duty to train up their children should tacitly shape how pastors discuss the children's ministry programs. Pastors should routinely emphasize parental responsibility and programming's ancillary role, and this should naturally pop up in the weekly interactions between pastors and their congregations. From time to time it should be addressed directly from the pulpit as well.

This truth can be communicated gently yet firmly by including it in new members' classes, where expectations for church involvement are set. By weaving this message into sermons and workshops, pastors can inspire parents to take their spiritual responsibility seriously without feeling overwhelmed or judged.

In the training for new leaders and children's ministry volunteers, the purpose of the ministries and their relationship to parents and the church should be plainly stated. Whenever the leaders and volunteers of the church meet to review the congregation's mission and strategy, this should be foregrounded and never assumed; whatever is assumed in an organization is lost, and the pressure to revert to prioritizing the programs as the way to disciple kids is always lurking. Pastors must articulate this consistently so that the staff, elders, and congregation internalize it.

Pastors must regularly affirm that while programs like Sunday school, VBS, and youth group are helpful tools, they are dispensable when it comes to the church's life. What is indispensable is a church culture that reinforces the importance of parental influence, intergenerational relationships, and intentional faith formation. Programs should never become the tail wagging the dog. When pastors emphasize that programs are routes taken to fulfill the church's vision and biblical convictions rather than being essential to that vision, sacred cows become less sacred and easier to slaughter when necessary.

This message is most clearly reinforced with staffing. How churches spend their money communicates their values—when staff hires and job descriptions prioritize discipling parents and ensuring that programs reinforce parental influence, the message gets across and is far easier to internalize as part of the congregation's culture.

Be Relaxed and Have High Standards in Children's and Youth Curriculum

When it comes to youth group especially, the current debate is where children's ministries should land on the spectrum of fun to studious. What should be clear at this juncture is that where churches land on this spectrum isn't as important as how children relate to the church as a whole. Often the intensity of this debate operates with the unspoken assumption that it is in Sunday school or youth group that children are truly discipled and their faith formation is really locked in, so the content is vitally important. But since it is parental influence and incorporation into the larger life of the church that is truly valuable, the curriculum and content of children's ministry programs are less pressing. So relax.

That being said, if these programs are to be both effective channels for parental influence and missionary outposts to a non-Christian world, then having a programmatic culture that reflects the values of the church and the best means of passing down the faith is necessary. The programs should mirror the kind of parenting style that is effective in handing down the faith: warm with high expectations.[5]

Gimmicks or overly shallow programming should be abandoned in favor of biblical teaching that reinforces knowing God as the ultimate goal. If the content of a children's ministry is biblical and doctrinally sound, it will help young participants see the sincerity of the church's faith and learn to take it seriously. Kids should be challenged to engage deeply with Scripture and understand the essentials of Christian doctrine. Holding them to high expectations in this area communicates that their faith is important, worth their effort, and something they are capable of understanding even at a young age. Theologian and pastor Sinclair Ferguson once commented to me that one of the values of having Bible teaching like this is that it provides scaffolding in the mind, so when the Word is preached the worshiper is better able to hold on to its meaning. This is true for both adults and kids and should be the aim of any children's ministry channeling.

At the same time, the form of these programs should embody warmth and joy. A warm, welcoming environment shows kids that they are not just attendees but valuable members of the church community. Leaders and volunteers should make it clear that children are liked and appreciated, greeting them with joy and friendliness. Just as authoritative parenting blends love with confident guidance, leaders in these ministries should also be humbly confident in addressing kids' questions and doubts about faith. Creating a space where curiosity is welcomed and questions are thoughtfully answered helps build trust and encourages spiritual growth. By holding kids to high expectations in their understanding of Scripture, providing a warm and welcoming environment, and deeply connecting them to the life of the church, these programs can serve as powerful tools for faith formation.

For kids and teens who come into these programs from outside the church, especially non-Christians, being welcomed and embraced is crucial. And for their sake, the content of children's programs should clearly teach them the gospel, the content of the Bible, and chief articles of the Christian faith. Particularly for non-Christian teenagers, who typically show up at youth groups because they want to be with their friends and are curious about the faith, a sincere, clear, confidently humble presentation of the faith is essential if the ministry will function in a missionary capacity and not just as a social activity. This is the only way the "necessary" aspect of Charlotte Mason's lament for Sunday school can actually be met.

The structure of these programs should organically connect to the rest of the life of the church, especially worship, so that unchurched kids can be incorporated into the means by which God saves and builds up. However, even while children's ministries can serve as a safety net for those exploring faith, reaching out to their parents is ultimately more effective. In the long term, the non-Christian kid's faith is best served if their parents embrace a vibrant Christianity, so the structure of the programming should be designed to allow the church to establish relationships with their families if possible.

Confirmation: An Invitation to a Deeper Faith

Not all churches have confirmation or its equivalent, but all churches have children who transition into adults, and that growth changes their relationship to the church. Whether it's confirmation or a high school graduation ceremony or passively doing nothing, churches have some form of dealing with this transition. Kids grow up and enter a new phase of life, and this presents both an opportunity and a danger for the church, which are represented by confirmation.

Confirmation is the traditional, intentional process by which adolescents fully confess and affirm the faith, typically by participating in a class and then being presented to the congregation. Its timing and significance varies from church to church, but it is a long-standing and venerable practice across most historical denominations.

Confirmation stands as a double-edged sword in the life of the church. When viewed merely as a requirement for "graduation," it risks becoming a milestone to check off rather than a meaningful encounter with faith and community. This is one of the chief dangers Christian Smith identified with the tradition of confirmation and others like it.[6] The risk is that, in the minds of kids, confirmation is reduced to a box to check to appease parents or tradition rather than a significant step in spiritual formation. When young people see confirmation this way, it can unintentionally facilitate their exit from the church by signaling the completion of their involvement rather than a deepening of their commitment. Many churches have experienced the sorrow of watching their church-confirmed kids become church-graduated adults.

However, when done well, confirmation becomes a transformative rite of passage that draws young people deeper into the life of the church. It is an opportunity to affirm their faith, nurture their spiritual maturity, and welcome them as active participants in the body of Christ. Through thoughtful preparation, confirmation can help young people see themselves as integral members of the church for their whole lives instead of a short season. This rite of passage can shape their identity as individuals whose faith is not merely inherited but lived and owned.

When approached with intentionality, confirmation can be pivotal in a young person's spiritual formation. To prevent it from being seen as a graduation from religious life, the church must deliberately frame it as a step toward deeper engagement with the faith community. This begins with re-thinking how confirmation is discussed and practiced. Leaders and parents should avoid language that implies it is the culmination of religious obligations. Instead, they can emphasize its role as a starting point for lifelong faith and active participation in the church. Much like with my experience as a five-year-old newly allowed to sit in the worship service, when confirmation is treated as an admission to the next phase of discipleship, which involves affirmation as a full member of the life of the church, teens-turned-adults rise to the expectations.

One of the best ways to avoid making confirmation a graduation from the church is to maintain the connection between faith and church membership. In my Presbyterian tradition, confirmation is historically tied to admission to the Lord's Supper, but not automatically, since we believe that a sincere profession of faith is necessary to receive the Eucharist. Since we view the children of Christians as parties to the covenant community, we treat them as members of the church even before they express faith. Our church does confirmation class for twelve-to-fourteen-year-olds, timed for kids transitioning from childhood toward adulthood. Confirmation (or communicant) classes serve as the intentional time when the kids of the church receive a focused education in order to be provided with the biblical vocabulary for their faith, so they may make a sincere profession of faith in Jesus if they have not done so already. That means the content of the class is an overview of the central beliefs and practices of the church, their biblical foundation, and how these truths interact with the questions the students have about faith and life. We are confirming the kids' faith so they may commune with the rest of the church as full members. This is not a graduation but a rite of passage that maintains the church's foundation of faith in the grace of God.

By emphasizing the need for personal faith and communicating clearly to both students and their parents that confirmation is intended to help them articulate where their faith lies, we defuse the pressure to complete the class as another box to be checked off. Even if kids do not yet profess faith in Christ, the pastors and elders have an improved sense of how to pray for and engage with them over the coming years. And none who decline to profess faith are ever run out of the church or treated as unwelcome.

Churches that do not have confirmation or its equivalent will still find significant value in designating an age range where kids receive a focused overview of the gospel and life in the church for the purpose of encouraging a profession of faith as a rite of passage. Stephen Smallman's *Understanding the Faith* is a great workbook and curriculum for preparing students to make a public profession of faith. While it is theologically Reformed, it is a good model for how such a class can effectively pass down the faith even for churches that don't hold to the Reformed understanding of the Christian faith. I always teach this class in my own church, and by having the pastor engaging the teens in a context with both high expectations and warmth, the kids feel comfortable raising their questions and skepticisms, which provides me with deeper insight into both their faith and the ways I can assist their parents in instructing them.

However a church goes about it, preparation for confirmation should reflect the purpose of integration into the life of the church by focusing on relational, experiential, and participatory aspects of faith. Classes and mentorship programs should not just teach doctrine but also immerse young people in the practices of the church, such as prayer, service, and worship. Pairing confirmands with adult mentors in the congregation can help them build meaningful connections and see examples of mature faith in action. Incorporating opportunities for service, whether within the church or in the broader community, reinforces the idea that confirmation marks a move toward active discipleship rather than passive membership.

During the confirmation service itself, the church can underline its significance as a rite of passage into adult participation. The liturgy should acknowledge the confirmands as full members of the church and charge them with the responsibilities of that role, particularly finding opportunities to serve alongside the other adults of the church. Involving the congregation in reaffirming support for the confirmands creates a sense of shared commitment and continuity. Confirmation is a time of admission and welcome, and the church should embrace the kids with open arms and expectations.

Youth Group and Sunday School: Channels for Parental Influence

Youth groups have long been staples of Christian ministry, serving as spaces where teenagers gather for lessons, games, worship, Bible study, and service projects.[7] The focus is often on fostering peer-to-peer relationships, with adult mentors providing guidance and oversight. While these elements can be beneficial, they must be properly subordinated to a more vital aim: reinforcing and extending parental influence in the spiritual formation of teenagers. Youth groups are most effective when they are intentionally connected to the broader church community and structured to facilitate meaningful relationships between young people and godly adults.

At their core, youth groups should not operate as isolated programs with the primary goal of offering teenagers their own unique space within the church. While peer friendships can provide support and camaraderie, they are not the primary vehicle for passing down lasting faith. Peer friendships are good, but if the point of the church's discipleship is to propagate the faith in a lasting way—and youth groups are to facilitate that—then the emphasis should rest on parental investment and youth-adult connection, not on teenagers having their own space.[8] We don't want them to have their own space; we want the church to be ours and theirs together.

To prioritize this intergenerational model, youth group gatherings should be held in settings that reflect the rhythms of family life rather than in classrooms or at events. Gathering in homes and around meals creates an environment that mirrors the warmth and intimacy of a family, fostering deeper relationships between youth and godly adults. When parents open their homes and include their children's peers in their spiritual and everyday lives, they model how faith is lived out in the context of ordinary relationships and routines. My teenage experiences with Gary and Patti's home and pancakes at my friend's house are good examples of this in action.

This approach requires a shift in mindset. Youth ministry must be viewed not as a siloed activity or independent entity but as an extension of parental influence and an integral part of the church's life. Parents should be central to this effort, supported by the wider church community. Godly adults within the church act as spiritual surrogate parents, reinforcing the faith foundations laid by parents and offering additional mentorship to fill any gaps. These relationships allow teenagers to see faith lived out in various contexts and provide them with a network of support and accountability.

There has been a notable drop in the pool of willing church volunteers over the past decade, with a corresponding rise in hand-wringing about how youth groups can recruit the necessary volunteers to keep functioning.[9] This anxiety is downstream of the status quo model that needs to be reworked. If churches prioritize parental influence and regular integration into church life, the issue of volunteers goes away, since the "volunteers" are just the families of the teens in the first place. And the risk of parent-led youth groups leading to parental burnout is minimized if the youth programs focus less on events and classes and more on sharing regular life as a community or hosting people in homes. Parents can still be invested and provide leadership in this way without attending every single teenage event.

Intergenerational connection is key. Teenagers need more than fun events and relatable leaders; they need to be woven into the fabric of church life. Such integration demonstrates that faith is not a compartmentalized activity but a shared journey within the family of God. It also counters the cultural narrative that isolates teenagers in their own separate worlds, offering them instead a vision of Christian community that is rich, supportive, and enduring. This doesn't rule out the "classic" setup of midweek gatherings and classes but informs how they should be established in relation to the rest of a church's approach to family discipleship.

Watermark Community Church, a large congregation in Dallas, implements this well through the development of middle school small groups. While they still have different age-focused events and classes, when students hit seventh grade, the church sorts them into sex-segregated small groups. These groups are then assigned two or three nonstaff older adults of the same gender who will lead and mentor this small group all the way through high school graduation—a six-year commitment! The teens and leaders establish a relationship that is warm and caring, along with high expectations for both parties, such that the leaders act as surrogate parents. These weekly meetings happen in the homes of the kids in the small groups on a rotating basis. This organically encourages the teens in the small groups to become friends not just with each other and their leaders but with the families of their peers; the small groups and their leaders reinforce, not replace, parental influence.

This specific model is an example of how "small church" culture and community can be effectively scaled up in larger congregations. It may not work at every church, but it is the kind of approach that prizes community over gimmicks in a way that channels parental influence.

Volunteers Need to Be Godly and Mature

This model also requires the surrogate parents to be mature and godly adults. One of the great disasters in American Christianity is putting young twenty-somethings in charge of youth and children's ministry. Peruse the websites and media for "next gen" ministries and conferences, and the youthful demographic of the ministry leaders will be alarmingly obvious. When I was a teenager myself, my dad once remarked that it was bizarre that churches would entrust its most vulnerable, immature, and critical members—children and teens—to people barely older than them, rather than to the wisest and most experienced members of the congregation.

As a result of the emphasis on teenagers needing to be led by someone "relatable," churches default to assigning the people most like the youth to lead them. This perpetuates the cycle, juvenilizing the American church,[10] and defies biblical wisdom. Teenagers need fathers and mothers and seasoned surrogate parents leading them, not twenty-two-year-old cool, older "cousins" filling that role. When "next gen" leaders investing in kids are basically the next generation themselves, the wheel has come off the cart. Young adults, many of whom by definition are newer and younger Christians, need to be led, not take the lead, in discipling the children of the church. Young adults often bring an energy and passion to youth ministry that is contagious, and churches are hard-pressed to justify turning down help. But strong, godly churches should absolutely say no to young adults leading the teens, instead directing them to serve in other areas or allowing them to serve under the guidance of older adults. That doesn't prohibit younger adults from serving teenagers as part of the larger community of the church, but they should not be the ones taking the lead if we want the faith to be passed down effectively.

After I graduated from college, I moved back to my hometown to attend seminary and returned to my childhood church and my old Boy Scouts program. I served as an assistant scoutmaster and chaplain for the troop, and some of the older scouts still there had been part of the troop when I was a scout myself. That was a good serving experience, but the fact that it was good training for me does not mean that it benefited the teenagers' faith retention. What made it good for the scouts was that Gordon and David, who were dads, were the real leaders. I led campfire devotionals, shared theological and biblical insights, and helped with some merit badges, but in no way was I the lead. The Scouts was an effective channel because the surrogate parents were fathers and experienced adults.

Since youth groups work best for passing down the faith if they major in having older, godly adults engaging with the kids, the staffing goal of the church should be to have "youth" ministers who focus on investing in and discipling the *parents* first. Staff may be necessary to coordinate events, classes, and teaching for the teens, but the key focus should be on ensuring that parents are strengthened for raising their kids. When this is downplayed and blended with the adult leaders' prolonged adolescence and a programmatic-centered approach to the youth, the parents themselves are disserved and have their maturity stymied.

As a pastor, I was once asked to lead a youth group that, despite some intergenerational, parental emphasis, was activity driven so that the kids had their own place. One parent, who had been deeply involved but no longer had any kids in the program, kept attending—ostensibly for the sake of the teens, but really because they preferred the juvenile ethos to the standards of adult discipleship. When they finally switched from attending youth group (as a back-row watcher!) to an adult Bible study and prayer group, this fifty-five-year-old panicked. Trading the fun and whimsy of youth group for adult spiritual expectations gave them anxiety attacks. This parent had never grown up.

Any ministry leader charged with overseeing teenage discipleship needs to prioritize strengthening parents to grow into mature godliness.[11] This is primarily done, whether by staff or especially by volunteers, by setting an example. The adults who should be intentionally recruited to host, teach kids, and disciple other parents are those who can be pointed to as examples of success: This is what a mature, godly adult is like; imitate them.[12] This is what successful, godly parenting looks like; be around them and become like them. The immature need the mature to become mature themselves (oxygen masks!). By definition, this precludes putting the youngest adults in positions to be leading teenagers and their parents.

By prioritizing relationships with spiritually mature adults and embedding youth ministry into the greater life of the church, we create the conditions for lasting faith formation. Programs and activities still have a place, but only when they serve this greater goal. Ultimately, the goal of youth ministry is not to entertain *or even to instruct*; it's to pass down the faith in a way that roots teenagers deeply in Christ and in the life of his body, the church.

Most of these principles also apply to children in elementary school or pre-K. As the various studies on secularism demonstrated, even while this age range is important for passing down the faith, it is in the crucial period of entering adolescence that churches need to ensure children are being properly discipled for long-term faith retention.

The applications to this younger cohort are similarly straightforward: Programs like Sunday school, children's church, and VBS have minimal effect on faith retention, often distract congregations from wiser stewardship of resources, and can become counterproductive if they silo kids off from the regular rhythms and worship of the church. Yet they can be helpful as channels for spiritual formation if they reinforce rather than replace parental influence. The way that these early-age programs become effective is if the content aligns with the church's teaching and is sincerely, warmly communicated in an age-appropriate way and in a format that encourages cross-generational connection with the children's parents and other godly adults.

As your church communicates new ministry objectives to the congregation, be sure to emphasize gratitude for the faithful people who have volunteered to teach and serve the kids of the church. That is a godly and virtuous commitment and should be honored, and children's ministries more than any other include adults who have joyously labored for years to teach and love children in arenas that entail special patience, sensitivity, and often thankless work. The church should clearly express appreciation for their service, never brusquely dismissing their volunteering as counterproductive.

Churches should seek to ensure that anyone who is teaching knows the faith and is a regular presence in the life of the kids and the church. Throwing warm bodies into classes to serve kids is a recipe for undermining faith retention.

Because things like Sunday school tend to be more of a class than the more informal dynamic of teenagers being hosted at someone's house, parental involvement should extend to teaching only if the parents are spiritually equipped for it. Too often kids' ministries assume that any Christian can teach the Bible to kids, which is a disaster in the making. It is the older, godly adults who should be present and leading. Like with youth groups, young adults should not be the ones taking the lead but should be assisting the older adults, and this is another way that the children can be incorporated into the life of the church. None of this is to devalue the efforts of earnest people who have poured their time and hearts into Sunday schools and children's ministries. It's because the work they are doing of discipling children is so valuable that it's worth doing it right, even if it means a significant course correction in the church's practice.

Faith retention is ultimately secured not by the strength of church programs but by the depth of parental and communal investment in a child's spiritual life. This requires the church to put first things first—prioritizing a culture where parents are discipled, children are deeply known in the life of the church, and programs exist to foster these relationships rather than function as isolated efforts. When connected to the broader life of the church, structured to invite children into deeper faith and led by mature, godly adults—whether parents or spiritual mentors—these programs can be valuable tools. However, the true task of pastors and church leaders is not to build faith through programming alone but to cultivate an ecosystem where lifelong discipleship is nurtured through relationships, with the cart of programming following the horse of parental investment.

Chapter 7

HOLDING ON
Ministering for Faith Beyond Childhood

One of my theological mentors was a great example of authoritative parenting, and yet two of his three adult children in no way considered themselves to be or lived as Christians. Once I asked him and his wife what they thought about this, and their response was to point to their kids' baptisms. This was not a desperate naivete of the sort when a parent recalls that their kid once said the sinner's prayer, and therefore it meant that no matter how they lived their life and what their belief was, they were actually saved. No, when they pointed to the baptism of their children, they were pointing to the reminder of God's promise: "Turn to me in faith, and I will be a God to you and your children." Their baptism is a permanent reminder of God's promise to freely offer salvation. They were children of the covenant, and that would never change. Were they Christians? Not in any real sense, but the gift of baptism was a blessed comfort to their parents that

God had already acted in their lives and marked them as his own, and he wasn't done with them yet. They may have wandered from the faith, but their story is not over.

This is true whether the kids were baptized as babies or baptized based upon their profession of faith and later abandoned Christianity. The great dechurching has come for the children of all Christian denominations.

And the great dechurching underscores the reality confronting many anxious parents: They can do everything right, or think they did, and their kids still may not remain followers of Jesus. Pastors will inevitably encounter both ashamed and anxious parents who are worried for their children. This anxiety, whether or not a child has walked away from the faith, prompts a series of questions that churches need to be prepared to compassionately answer. What role can parents and family play in faith retention for their now-adult children? What can the church do for the faith retention of its young adults? How should parents react to the promises of God when their kids walk away from the faith, and how can the church minister to them in that sorrow?

The hope of God's people lies in his grace for the kids who have grown. And like with conversion, God's gifts of the family and church have a role to play in building up the faith of adult children. Even when they have grown up, it's never too late and no one is ever too far gone from the grace of God. The long-term outcomes of child-to-adult faith retention rely upon the same principles as when that faith was instilled in the first place.

Parental influence remains the strongest factor in whether these adult children eventually return to the faith, with grandparents also playing a significant role. If pastors and churches desire to see young adults hold on to their faith—and to equip parents to exercise their lasting influence effectively—they must first understand why some kids walk away. This requires a solid biblical and theological foundation to guide both pastoral care and practical action. It also demands insight into how parents can continue to nurture faith in their grown children, as well as concrete steps churches can take to help young adults navigate the transition into mature Christian adulthood. Ultimately, pastors must support these young people and also minister to the parents of prodigals, offering them wisdom, encouragement, and the hope found in Christ.

Why Kids Walk Away

One of the most straightforward ways this transition away from faith occurs is when young adults stop identifying as Christian altogether. They no longer claim the label of Christianity, whether in surveys, conversations, or personal reflections. They may not be hostile to Christianity, but they don't care about it anymore. This is related to but distinct from another significant shift, when kids cease to live according to Christian teachings, particularly in areas like regular church attendance, prayer, and engagement with Scripture. While they might still consider themselves Christians in some sense, their lives no longer reflect active participation in the faith community or adherence to its practices. This drift often coincides with entering college or the workforce, where routines and priorities change.

Perhaps the most profound change occurs in those who undergo a process of deconstruction or deconversion. This involves reevaluating their beliefs, questioning long-held assumptions, and ultimately rejecting the faith they were raised in. This process is often influenced by exposure to new ideas, challenges to their worldview, or personal experiences that seem incompatible with their previous understanding of Christianity. The movement from living under the rules and authority of Christian parents, where their beliefs were the default in a pluralistic world full of good people, is often the force at play here. The internet, with its wealth of information and diverse perspectives, often plays a significant role in accelerating this process.

My observation is that kids who are told they need to be a Christian in order to be a good person are most vulnerable to deconstruction. When they enter into a world full of non-Christians who are good people living fulfilled lives, many of whom are nicer than the Christians they know, it places into sharp relief the moral reasoning of their faith and invites a serious reexamination of it. Mitigating this goes beyond parents and churches being transparent about sin, grace, and repentance (and therefore addressing hypocrisy) and requires getting the gospel right: Yes, Jesus sanctifies his people and they should improve morally, but the reason to be a Christian is to be rescued from sin and called into the fellowship of Jesus. In many cases, these doubts and questions were already present during adolescence but were suppressed or unnoticed until the individual gained independence from parental oversight. It is this category of deconstruction and ceasing to believe that most people refer to when they speak of young adults leaving the faith. It represents a deep and often painful break from their religious upbringing.

Theologically, there are three ways we should understand why young adults raised as Christians might leave the faith. One perspective is that these kids never had genuine saving faith to begin with. While they were part of the covenant community, they were never truly united to Christ by faith. Their outward participation masked an inward lack of trust and transformation. As John writes, "They went out from us, but they were not of us; for if they had been of us, they would have continued with us" (1 John 2:19). As soon as the parental obligation to participate in the life of the church was lifted, they were able to act according to their true convictions. The good news here, of course, is that Jesus saves sinners, even sinners who grew up in church.

A second dimension is that belief is not a static state but a dynamic one. Many deconversion stories involve kids who sincerely believed in Christ during their youth but later moved away from that belief. These were not people who faked their faith or even deceived themselves. They truly believed in Jesus and the tenets of the Christian faith. This understanding carries two significant implications. First, while saving faith is rational, its essence is trust in Christ, not intellectual assent or sheer willpower. Faith rests upon Christ as he is offered in the gospel, which means that someone's earlier belief, even if it later fades, was not nonexistent simply because it didn't endure. Their belief was genuine in that it was rational and honestly held in the mind, but it was not a faith that truly rested upon Christ; the person's mind and emotions may have been in the right spot, but they were never regenerated by the Holy Spirit. The second implication is that just as belief can waver or change during young adulthood, so it is not permanently fixed in a current state of unbelief for a young adult. The fact that someone no longer believes now does not mean they are beyond the reach of God's grace. The sincerity of earlier belief and its current absence are both part of a larger spiritual journey.

The third theological lens is the story of the prodigal son, which offers hope for those who have wandered away from the faith. Many young adults enter phases of life where they become skeptical, disengaged, or entangled in sin. Yet the parable of the prodigal son (Luke 15:11–32) reminds us that God's grace is always available, and those who stray can return. The parable has two key implications for the hope of faith retention by our wandering kids. First, the son who abandons his father remains his son the entire time he is gone. While "prodigal" is the word most associated with this story and has become culturally synonymous with "wandering," it actually means something like "reckless and wasteful extravagance." The younger son was a prodigal because he recklessly and wastefully handled his father's blessing and relationship. Some of the kids who walk away from the faith are still Christians—wastefully squandering the blessings of their relationship with their heavenly Father, perhaps, but still united to Jesus by faith. But true union with Christ requires that, like the son in the parable, they return. The father celebrates the son's return as if he had been lost and dead (Luke 15:32) because relationally, that was what he was to his dad—estranged. And living estranged from God is as if we're lost and dead to him. Returning in repentance is what restores us to life through God's grace. The good news for parents of prodigals is that God specializes in finding the lost and raising the dead, and no one is beyond his reach.

The studies that have examined why kids who grew up Christian left the faith (in contradistinction to the studies examining why they stayed) support these three broad descriptions. The kids who were raised in authoritarian, permissive, or passive homes were only in church because they were compelled to be there. Once that authority structure was removed, the kids flew the coop.

Many parents do their best to protect their children from the sinful influences of the world—and they should! But sometimes that protection manifests in unhealthy ways, with the values and currents of the world unacknowledged and the curiosity of the kids met with dismissals. When parents impatiently or thoughtlessly pass over their kids' questions and objections, they don't prepare them for life outside the home. The faith of a child is like a tree; unless smaller winds blow on them to strengthen their resistance, they will collapse when the big storms hit.

Kids need to have the doubts and questions of their faith met lovingly and directly to build their resolve. They need to practice deconstructing (i.e., examining and evaluating and questioning their faith) alongside their parents and the church so their faith can survive contact with the world.[1] When adult children are confronted with values and beliefs contrary to their faith, going to authoritarian parents who won't take the substance of their growing skepticism seriously is not viewed as an option, and asking for help from permissive or passive parents who don't really care about the difference between Christian doctrine and the world is unhelpful.

Additionally, what all the walking away from Christianity has in common is a young adult's disconnection from the routine and community of faith upon entering into adulthood.[2] When there is a significant shift in life after high school, especially when a young adult either moves or begins college, the disruption leaves them vulnerable to making a lack of faith practices habitual.

What Can Pastors Do to Help Parents?

Parents remain a crucial influence on faith retention for their children, even after the kids enter into adulthood and approach their thirties. This extends beyond the trajectory the parents set their kids on when they were children to the relationship between them now that the kids are grown up. Parents' influence on their children's faith continues to have a profound impact, regardless of whether the children maintain their Christian identity or walk away from it. Pastors need to understand this dynamic in order to better instruct parents to positively influence their adult children.

For children who remain Christian, the ongoing relationship with their parents plays a vital role in reinforcing their faith. All the positive effects of their parents' sincere, routine faith in their childhood continue to positively affect them into adulthood. This also means that just as parents should pursue a lively Christian walk when they have kids at home for the sake of their kids, they should continue to do so when their kids have grown up. In one sense, parents are freed from their kids once the kids are grown because they don't have to raise them, so their schedule is much more flexible. But when parents take this freedom to mean that they can pull back from engagement with the church ("I did my time!") or let church attendance and routine faith bow to other priorities like vacations or weekend getaways, it communicates to their kids that faith was just part of the menu of childcare options that expired once the kids were grown. In other words, it teaches their adult children, still, that faith and church are things from which you graduate, just perhaps at a later date than high school. Ongoing faithfulness on the part of parents reinforces the faith of their adult children.

For kids who walk away from Christianity, parental influence is often a determining factor in whether they eventually return.[3] The foundation laid in childhood, combined with the continued presence of the parents' faith, can create a space for reconsideration and renewal. The nature of this influence hinges on the parents' approach to their relationship with their adult children. The authoritative style of parenting that fosters faith retention in childhood is effective into adulthood, though adapted for an adult relationship. While authoritative parenting in childhood involves setting boundaries and enforcing expectations, when children become adults, the focus shifts from exercising parental authority to offering wise and experienced guidance. Gentle pushing and reminders of expectations and the standards for Christian behavior for continued engagement in faith practices can remain helpful, but in the changed dynamic, the emphasis should be on warmth.

Parents who can maintain a sincere, confident, and routine faith while extending warmth—even to children who have left the faith—create an environment of trust. When adult children feel they can approach their parents without fear of judgment or rejection, they are more likely to remain open to conversations about faith. Do the children trust that their parents will listen to their experiences and questions without dismissiveness? When kids bring up negative childhood faith experiences, will they trust their parents to be humble and open to the criticisms, even if the parents don't ultimately agree with them? Will the parents demonstrate care and love regardless of their children's current beliefs or choices? This does not mean acceptance or endorsement; it means the same kind of warmth and patience given to the child when they were a toddler or teenager, though expressed in an age-appropriate way. Even into adulthood this is what helps kids hold on to and return to the faith.

Encouragingly, parents who fell short during their children's upbringing can still make a positive impact. Even if they were authoritarian, permissive, passive, or non-Christian parents when their kids were young, they can adopt an authoritative approach now. By embracing sincerity, warmth, and a listening ear, they can rebuild trust and foster an environment conducive to their children retaining or turning to faith. You never stop being a parent, which means that even empty nesters can continue learning how to parent.

However, there are pitfalls that need to be avoided in navigating the parent–adult child relationship, particularly in the context of faith. One common danger is reverting to the dynamics of the parent-child relationship from earlier years. Parents must remember that their children are now adults with their own autonomy. Attempting to assert control, dismiss their skepticism, or dictate their faith journey is likely to backfire, pushing them further away. Respecting their independence while maintaining a supportive presence is crucial. While it's important to hold firmly to one's own beliefs and remind kids how they were raised and what being part of God's family entails, these must be tempered with warmth. Harsh criticism or inflexibility can erode the trust necessary for meaningful conversations. Parents should aim to model a faith that is both confident and compassionate, demonstrating how belief is lived out rather than imposed.

For evangelical parents, the interplay of faith and politics often presents an additional challenge. While specific political positions or allegiances do not significantly affect faith retention, the marriage of faith and politics can create tension that undermines the parent-child relationship. As young adults mature, they often begin to question not only religious assumptions but also political ones. This questioning can lead to intergenerational disagreements as political beliefs inherited from parents are reevaluated in light of new perspectives. These arguments are a normal part of family dynamics and are a staple of Thanksgiving dinners, as anyone who has attended one with parents and their college students can attest. But they still require careful navigation.

The real danger arises when parents treat political questioning or changes in political positions as equivalent to religious apostasy. This conflation can escalate disagreements and cause lasting harm to the parent-child relationship. On the other hand, though many Christian parents are often careful to make sure they don't push their adult children too hard on religion, they don't show the same restraint with political debates, in part because those are less important. This leads to a greater willingness to debate and be confrontational since the risks to faith retention seem lower. However, if the parents' politics and religion are intertwined, this will still be counterproductive. Political debates, while often passionate, should not bleed into discussions about faith in ways that alienate or antagonize adult children. For parents who are deeply politically invested, it is essential to approach disagreements with the same warmth and openness required for faith transmission. Abrasive or dismissive arguments can damage the trust necessary for fruitful faith discussions. Like conversations and debates about the Christian faith, political conversations should be carried out warmly.

Parents can also be good grandparents. While a grandparent's influence is much smaller than a parent's, their faith and presence will still positively impact their grandchildren.[4]

When grandparents have an authoritative style, clear boundaries, warmth, and sincere faith, their grandkids are better off. Being involved in the lives of their adult children as helpers with the grandkids is a good way to pass along their faith to the grandkids and to communicate warmth and dependability to their own kids. When grandkids have believing parents, the genuine Christian faith of their grandparents is one of the greatest means of reinforcing parental influence. Even when the grandkids have unbelieving parents, grandparental influence is beneficial for passing along the faith. If parents allow for it, grandparents can step into the spiritual role that parents should have, such as teaching the faith, inviting grandkids to worship, and channeling their faith through other activities.

How the Church Can Help During the Transition into Adulthood

The church's role in faith retention for young adults is primarily to be a source of continuity between their childhood and adulthood. Churches that intentionally integrate young people into the full life of the congregation, rather than treating youth ministries as separate silos, help bridge the gap between teenage faith and adult discipleship.

One of the most significant ways churches can encourage faith retention is by ensuring that young people are deeply connected to the community of the church before they graduate from high school. If teens' primary experience of worship and discipleship is limited to age-segregated environments, transitioning to "adult" church often feels jarring and unappealing. This disconnection can make it challenging for them to set down roots in their home church upon graduation or to engage with new congregations when they move away for college or work.

Young adults who stay local after high school and enter the workforce or trades often face a unique challenge. Without the structure of college life or peer-based campus ministries, their connection to the church can weaken as their high school social circles dissolve. While it is not a geographic move that disrupts their continuity with past faith routines, the change in life stage and the relationship to their parents and church often has the same effect for this easily forgotten demographic. Though things like young adult groups can be helpful for keeping them connected to a specific congregation, churches often find themselves prioritizing focus on the "college and career" twenty-somethings to the neglect of the eighteen-to-twenty-five-year-old McDonald's workers. If the goal is faith retention, integration into the life of the church so that faith continues to be valued is key. A particular way this integration can occur is by including high school students in adult small groups long before they turn eighteen. This can look different for each congregation, but my experience with Gary and Patti is a good example of this kind of seamless transition.

The movement of young adults heading to college often disrupts faith retention due to new routines and environments. The authors of *The Great Dechurching* found that a whopping 19 percent of evangelicals who dechurched said they did so because they moved and didn't find a new congregation.[5] Young adults are particularly vulnerable to this danger. Churches can help mitigate this disruption by being proactive. When students leave home, they often face uncertainty about where to worship. Pastors can take an active role by recommending sound and compatible local churches easily accessible from the student's college. While it's sometimes time-consuming, I provide two to five ranked recommendations with pros and cons for every student in my church who goes off to college. This allows them to make an informed choice without being overwhelmed, but they are the ones making the decision. If I know the pastor at the church and the student is okay with it, I make introductions between them.

Something similar should happen in recommending campus ministries. Campus ministries play a pivotal role in engaging college students and providing them a pool of trustworthy peers. Pastors should investigate campus ministries with philosophies that align with their own (and, since there is variety within the same ministries, investigate the particular staff at each one) and encourage students to get involved. For long-term faith retention, the campus ministries that prioritize integrating students into the local church are best. It should not be assumed that all campus ministries do this; the ones that do it best are typically sponsored by local churches and are associated with a denomination. Campus ministries are good, but the church is the body of Christ, and connection to the church is essential in faith retention. Campus ministries should reinforce the discipleship of the church, not supplant it. Prioritizing ministries that point students toward the local church ensures they remain connected to the broader body of Christ and protects continuity with the faith of their youth. As with connecting to the pastors of local churches, connecting students to campus ministers is a great way to ensure that in the shuffle of moving and settling into school, someone local knows them and is looking out for them.

For college students who remain in the area, similar campus ministry recommendations are helpful, and like with graduates who go directly into the workforce, continued integration into the community of the church is key. Congregations should never assume that discipleship is taking place on campus or outsource to campus ministries their responsibility to their confirmed members. Campus ministries are partners with, not replacements for, the ordinary means of grace.

Graduates entering military service often face a difficult challenge of staying connected to their faith due to the transient and demanding nature of military life. Pastors can encourage them to connect with chaplains in their units, and once they are stationed at a base, pastors can help them identify good local churches.

One of the most critical steps churches can take is to treat young adults as adults, not as an extension of their parents. Respecting their independence while offering high standards of discipleship communicates care and trust. Following up directly with young adults—rather than relying on their parents or lumping them in together when doing shepherding check-ins—not only *shows* that the church values them as individuals but *is* valuing them as individuals.

Maintain those relationships and encourage the broader community of older adults in the church to keep up the connections they forged with the youth. For those young adults who are local and still living with their parents, pastors connecting with them directly is essential. Like with parents, I have found that meeting young adults and asking them what their plan is to intentionally grow in their Christian walk is an easy way to spark their self-motivation for remaining connected to the church.

For young adults who have moved, either for school or for work, continuing to follow up with them in genuine interest until they become members of a new home church helps maintain a sense of home and continuity in addition to high expectations for them as adults. For young adults who return home for the holidays or summer, taking them out to coffee or lunch is invaluable. If a college student's campus isn't too far away, pastors making the trip to visit with them and encourage them is another key way of supporting them in the faith.

Hope for Ashamed and Anxious Parents

Conversion happens by faith and covenant. Sometimes parents are terrible, and by the grace of God he saves their children anyway. Sometimes parents are wonderful and do everything so right that it's not even "doing" something but just the very essence of their home life, and their kids do not come to faith in Jesus. And sometimes kids don't stay Christian, and the failure of their parents to raise them well is the worldly cause of their not remaining in the faith.

All three of these are common realities in the church. Pastors have a key role in addressing parents who have come through these situations by bringing the gospel to bear on their lives.

We have the reminder that salvation is always by God's sovereign grace. We live in a fallen world, and doing everything right does not change the arithmetic of salvation. We may have been the very best parents, but that does not save our children. When we do everything right as parents, we are just stewarding God's blessings well; he works through the normal means of family and church, but salvation is still his gift and prerogative to deliver. We need to entrust our kids to our Father and his provision of salvation through Jesus by the Spirit.

When we fail, God's grace is powerful. He can work despite our parental failures and save our children. If we did wrong by our kids and they are still in the church, we should be reminded that God worked for their salvation despite our missteps. If we are to serve the church as positive models, we must confront our mistakes through repentance and striving to do better. And when we fail and our kids do not stay Christian, God's grace—the work of Jesus to save *us* from our sin and sorrow—remains our hope. God remains our only hope in life and death, blessing and sorrow, and we need to place the affliction of our kids walking away from the faith in his hands.

And we continue to trust the grace of God for our kids. The Holy Spirit goes where he wills, and the children of God are born not of blood but through the blood of Jesus and faith in him. When the sorrow of our children departing from Christianity confronts us, whether or not we did our best when they were kids, there is nothing better to place our hope in than the grace of God. His grace and purposes cannot be thwarted and will prevail. Our children's stories are not done, and God is at work. Because of this, prayer for our children can and should characterize our lives.[6]

The hope that the church can provide parents is not the promise that God will assuredly save their children, but that assuredly God is almighty, gracious, and abounding in steadfast love. Parents of prodigals can trust that God is good and that the gospel of grace remains true even when the kids they love have wandered from the faith.

CONCLUSION

Built to Last: Discipleship for a Lifetime

Dechurching and deconversion are not inevitable, and God has given his people great gifts to ensure that the faith of his saints is passed down to them: their parents in their natural family and all the means of grace in the church, God's family of grace.

While salvation is ultimately the work of God, the means through which faith is nurtured—family, corporate worship, community, and discipleship—are given by God as essential instruments in sustaining belief from childhood into adulthood. This book has explored the key elements of lifelong discipleship, identifying the most solid ways for churches and families to instill a resilient, deeply rooted faith in the next generation. As we conclude, it is essential to step back and examine the overarching principles that emerge from these discussions and their implications for churches and parents seeking to fulfill this calling.

At the heart of Christian discipleship is the understanding that children are already part of the covenant community. The church does not wait for them to profess faith before treating them as Christians; rather, it nurtures them as believers from the beginning. This orientation shapes every aspect of how the church and family approach discipleship, ensuring that children grow up with an understanding of belonging rather than feeling like outsiders who must earn their place. This conviction reorients the way parents and pastors view their responsibility: cultivating and calling their children to faith in the covenant promises of God, to which they are heirs. Reliance upon the means of grace that God has given—his Word, prayer in worship, and the sacraments—is the single most effective philosophy of ministry for creating lifelong disciples of Jesus.

The greatest influential factor in a child's retention of faith is their parents. This parental responsibility is best fulfilled through an authoritative parenting style—one that balances firm boundaries with warmth and affection. Children are most likely to embrace the faith when they experience it as integral to their home life, reinforced by loving parental guidance rather than detached rule setting. Parents who model a sincere, all-encompassing faith—one that is evident in their daily lives, decisions, and priorities—are the most successful in passing it on to their children. Churches, in turn, must recognize this reality and orient their ministries toward equipping parents for this task rather than assuming the burden of discipleship themselves.

Pastors and church leaders play a crucial role in shaping the spiritual culture of both families and the congregation. They do this not merely through teaching and programming but through example—by modeling discipleship, parenting, and leadership in their own lives. When church leaders live out the faith with visible joy, patience, and integrity, they provide a pattern for families to follow. In this way, the pastoral role extends beyond the pulpit and into the daily lives of the congregation, influencing what people believe and how they live out their faith within their families. Because of this, pastors must prioritize faith formation in the home rather than rely primarily on church programs. Their greatest impact comes from equipping and supporting parents to fulfill their God-given role as the primary shapers of their children.

A vital yet often overlooked aspect of lifelong discipleship is the incorporation of children into gathered worship. Rather than segregate them into separate programs or accommodate them in ways that diminish their participation, the church should fully incorporate children into the worshiping life of God's people. Worship is formative, and children learn to love what their parents and community cherish. When children are included in the church's worship, they are more likely to develop a lasting affection for it. This requires intentionality from pastors and congregations, who must resist the temptation to prioritize convenience over spiritual formation. More broadly, churches must restructure their ministry to integrate children and youth into the full life of the congregation, ensuring that they experience belonging within the intergenerational church family.

Beyond worship, children's faith is best nurtured within the full life of the church rather than through isolated programs. While youth group and Sunday school have their place, they should never replace genuine intergenerational relationships within the church. Children need to be known and loved by a broad range of spiritually mature adults who model Christian living. This means that churches must resist the impulse to rely too heavily on structured programs at the expense of fostering a genuine, relational community. Programs are useful when they serve the greater goal of integrating children into the larger church family, but they become counterproductive when they function as substitutes for true community.

This prioritization of relationships over programs extends to the way churches allocate resources and structure their ministries. It is easy to assume that well-designed programs will ensure faith retention, but the reality is that faith is primarily transmitted through personal investment, especially by parents. When churches recognize this, they can structure their ministries to support parental discipleship rather than inadvertently replace it. The best programs are those that reinforce, rather than compete with, the influence of parents and the broader church community. By keeping the horse before the cart, churches can ensure that their ministries serve the deeper goal of faith retention rather than becoming ends in themselves. Ministry leaders must take a generational view, making long-term investments in faith formation rather than focusing solely on immediate results.

Even beyond childhood, the influence of parents and the church community remains critical in the faith journey of young adults. Many will experience seasons of doubt or drift away, but studies consistently show that those with strong parental and church connections are more likely to return. The church must, therefore, continue its ministry to both young adults and their parents, equipping families with wisdom and encouragement to maintain their spiritual influence. Additionally, pastors must be prepared to minister to parents of prodigals, offering them biblical encouragement with a deep and abiding hope in the faithfulness of Christ.

Ultimately, lifelong discipleship is not about guaranteeing outcomes but about faithfully receiving the means of grace that God has given. Parents, pastors, and church communities are called to create an environment where faith is nurtured through genuine relationships, joyful worship, and the consistent meditation upon God's Word. God has provided these ordinary things—family and grace together—as the foundation for sustaining faith. By realigning ministry priorities, churches can play a vital role in ensuring that children raised in the faith stay Christian for life.

While no method or program can replace the sovereign work of God in salvation, the church is responsible for cultivating the conditions in which faith can flourish. By prioritizing parental discipleship, fostering authentic community, incorporating children fully into worship, and ensuring that programs serve rather than lead, the church can better fulfill its mission of raising up the next generation of faithful believers. The calling of the church, the privilege of parents, and the hope of God's people is this: By his grace and the work of his Holy Spirit, our children will remain Christian and pass faith in Jesus Christ on to future generations.

ACKNOWLEDGMENTS

Keeping Kids Christian began as the article "How Our Kids Stay Christian" at *Mere Orthodoxy*, and I owe thanks to Jake Meador, who graciously ran it and helped set in motion the publication of this book. I'm also deeply indebted to Ginni Beam for generously giving her time and editorial skill to help shape the manuscript. I appreciate your friendship.

I'm grateful to the whole team at Baker, especially Eddie LaRow, Carrie Weston, Jessica English, and Ava DeVries, for guidance, patience, editorial direction, and commitment to getting the book from draft to publication.

Finally, my deepest thanks go to my wife, Lauren, whose support and patience in the hours it took this first-time author to get this thing done made it possible. I love you.

NOTES

Introduction

1. This concept is articulated by Aaron Renn as the "negative world" in *Life in the Negative World: Confronting Challenges in an Anti-Christian Culture* (Zondervan, 2024). Renn's thesis is that beginning roughly in 2014, being a Christian is, on balance, a social negative in the United States and that holding to traditional Christian moral views, particularly related to sex and gender, is seen as a threat to the public good and public moral order.

2. "How U.S. Religious Composition Has Changed in Recent Decades," Pew Research Center, September 13, 2022, https://www.pewresearch.org/religion/2022/09/13/how-u-s-religious-composition-has-changed-in-recent-decades/.

3. "'Nones' on the Rise: One-In-Five Adults Have No Religious Affiliation," Pew Research Center, October 9, 2012, https://web.archive.org/web/20140826234925/http://www.pewforum.org/files/2012/10/NonesOnTheRise-full.pdf.

4. Ryan P. Burge, *The Nones: Where They Came From, Who They Are, and Where They Are Going* (Fortress Press, 2021), 2; Ryan P. Burge, *The American Religious Landscape: Facts, Trends, and the Future* (Oxford University Press, 2025), 17.

5. Ryan Burge, "The Religion of America's Young Adults," Graphs About Religion, September 26, 2024, https://www.graphsaboutreligion.com/p/the-religion-of-americas-young-adults; Burge, *American Religious Landscape*, 233–35.

6. Jim Davis and Michael Graham with Ryan P. Burge, *The Great Dechurching: Who's Leaving, Why Are They Going, and What Will It Take to Bring Them Back?* (Zondervan, 2023).

7. Sarah McCammon's *The Exvangelicals: Loving, Living, and Leaving the White Evangelical Church* (St. Martin's, 2024) is an archetypal example.

8. It's worth noting that historically the church has grown primarily through demographics, not conversions. Rodney Stark's *The Rise of Christianity: How the Obscure, Marginal Jesus Movement Became the Dominant Religious Force in the Western World in a Few Centuries* (Harper, 1997) provides a good overview of this argument and was recently reexamined by Scott Alexander in "Book Review: The Rise of Christianity," Astral Codex Ten, November 12, 2024, https://www.astral codexten.com/p/book-review-the-rise-of-christianity.

9. Amy Adamczyk and Christian Smith, *Handing Down the Faith: How Parents Pass Their Religion on to the Next Generation* (Oxford University Press, 2021). Examples of research upon which Adamczyk and Smith built their work include Gordon Neufield and Gabor Maté's *Hold On to Your Kids: Why Parents Need to Matter More Than Peers* (Random House, 2006) and Vern L. Bengtson's *Families and Faith: How Religion Is Passed Down Across Generations* (Oxford University Press, 2017).

10. There are some similarities and overlap in this book, with the family-integrated approach well summarized in Randy Stinson and Timothy Paul Jones's *Trained in the Fear of God: Family Ministry in Theological, Historical, and Practical Perspective* (Kregel, 2011). However, the family-integrated approach begins with the idea of the church as the "family of families" (not a bad starting point!) and moves outward from there without much consideration of sociological observation. This book begins with parents and then moves toward the church, asking how the church can best support parents in raising faithful children in light of what is seen in both Scripture and culture.

Chapter 1 Born into God's Family

1. O. Palmer Robertson, *The Christ of the Covenants* (P&R Publishing, 1987), 4.

2. Douglas Gropp, "Divine Covenants and Treaties," Third Mill, accessed July 16, 2025, https://thirdmill.org/answers/answer.asp/file/46845.

3. *First Catechism: Teaching Children Bible Truths* (Great Commission Publications, 2003), 10. This is a modernized, child-friendly version of the Westminster Shorter Catechism.

4. I am an unapologetic Presbyterian on this point and believe that because of the spiritual and covenant nature of baptism, children of Christian parents should be baptized as infants. However, what I am saying here is true as well for families and churches that practice believers-only baptism. I myself grew up in a faithful Baptist household and was baptized at the age of nine. Baptism of children, regardless of the age or profession of personal faith, is a sign and seal of God's gospel promises and is a means to build up our children in their faith.

5. For more reading on this, see my article "You Must Be Baptized to Receive the Lord's Supper," *Mere Orthodoxy*, November 26, 2024, https://mereorthodoxy.com/baptism-eucharist.

Chapter 2 Faithful, Firm, and Fun

1. Lyman Stone, "Secularization Begins at Home," Institute for Family Studies, August 31, 2023, https://ifstudies.org/blog/secularization-begins-at-home.

2. Stone, "Secularization Begins at Home."

3. Ryan Burge also argues that the internet has been a significant factor in increased secularization since 1990 (Burge, *The Nones*, 47–56, 66).

4. Benjamin L. Mabry, "Losing Their Religion," review of *Nonverts* by Stephen Bullivant, *First Things*, August 1, 2023, https://www.firstthings.com/article/2023/08/losing-their-religion.

5. A consistent theme across all of these works on dechurching and the rise of the nones, but especially highlighted by Bullivant and Stone, is that the particular ideology of parents has very little bearing on long-term faith retention. A common refrain heard is that many ex-evangelical Christian kids left their tradition because of its affinity for Christian nationalism and anti-LGBTQ+ posture. Bullivant in particular demonstrates that this isn't the case, but that the dynamics of relational commitments and the preexisting sense of who is a friend or enemy leads Americans to construct and filter their political views. In other words, specific ethical positions or political affiliations have a negligible effect on dechurching, though perhaps they have reshuffled the preexisting affiliation of (ir)religious individuals.

6. "Church Dropouts: Reasons Young Adults Stay or Go Between Ages 18–22," Lifeway Research, January 15, 2019, https://research.lifeway.com/wp-content/uploads/2019/01/Young-Adult-Church-Dropout-Report-2017.pdf.

7. Adamczyk and Smith, *Handing Down the Faith*, 37–55.

8. Christian Smith, "Keeping the Faith," *First Things*, May 1, 2021, https://www.firstthings.com/article/2021/05/keeping-the-faith.

9. Traci Smith's *Faithful Families: Creating Sacred Moments at Home* (Chalice Press, 2017) and Danielle Hitchen's *Sacred Seasons: A Family Guide to Center Your Year Around Jesus* (Harvest House, 2023) have countless examples of how to do this well.

10. Adamczyk and Smith, *Handing Down the Faith*, 37–39; Davis, Graham, and Burge, *The Great Dechurching*, 9–10, 46–48, 150–55.

11. Tim Keller's *Forgive: Why Should I and How Can I?* (Viking, 2022) is an excellent guide on this subject.

12. Adamczyk and Smith, *Handing Down the Faith*, 48–50.

13. Davis, Graham, and Burge, *The Great Dechurching*, 46–48.

14. Adamczyk and Smith, *Handing Down the Faith*, 70–71. This isn't to say that kids should only ever interact with their parents or that kids don't need their own times and spaces (the "free-range kid" movement has demonstrated the value of developing childhood independence), but that disengagement in a kid's faith for the sake of not pressuring them is counterproductive.

Chapter 3 Leading by Example

1. Four good parenting books that align with an authoritative style include Justin Whitmel Early's *Habits of the Household: Practicing the Story of God in Everyday Rhythms* (Zondervan, 2021), Paul David Tripp's *Parenting: 14 Gospel Principles That Can Radically Change Your Family* (Crossway, 2024), Tedd Tripp's *Shepherding a Child's Heart* (Shepherd Press, 1995), and Melissa B. Kruger's *Parenting with Hope: Raising Teens for Christ in a Secular Age* (Harvest House, 2024).

2. This does not mean that pastor, elder, deacon, or other church leader candidates need to be married and have kids. Paul is explaining that *if* they have children, this is the requirement for leaders. This can be deduced not just from common sense but also from Paul's argument in 1 Corinthians 9:3–6 that he and the other apostles actually do have a right to be married (implying that they are not and do not have children) and that he and Barnabas set aside that right for the sake of their ministry.

3. Paul Raeburn, *Do Fathers Matter?: What Science Is Telling Us About the Parent We've Overlooked* (Scientific American, 2015); Go Woon Suh et al., "Effects of the Interparental Relationship on Adolescents' Emotional Security and Adjustment: The Important Role of Fathers," *Developmental Psychology* 52, no. 10 (October 2016): 1666–78, https://doi.org/10.1037/dev0000204.

4. Bengtson, *Families and Faith*, 71–98.

5. Vern Bengtson, as quoted in Mark Oppenheimer, "Book Explores Ways Faith Is Kept, or Lost, over Generations," *New York Times*, January

31, 2014, https://www.nytimes.com/2014/02/01/us/book-explores-ways -faith-is-kept-or-lost-over-generations.html.

6. A good example of this is the "Radical Mentoring" discipleship curriculum, which in its men's and dads' groups utilizes Ross Campbell's *How to Really Love Your Child* (David C Cook, 2015).

7. Daniel Silliman, "If You're a Christian, You Should Probably Thank Your Mom," *Christianity Today*, May/June 2024, https://www.christian itytoday.com/2024/04/mom-mother-faith-religious-transmission-study/.

8. A 2019 study by Barna found that Christian teenagers were more likely to talk with their mom (72%) about religious faith than their dad (55%) (*Households of Faith: The Rituals and Relationships That Turn a Home into a Sacred Space* [Barna Group, 2019], 109; see also "The Powerful Influence of Moms in Christians' Households," Barna, May 7, 2019, https://www.barna.com/research/moms-christians-households/).

9. Lyman Stone, "Want Your Kids to Stay Christian? Double Down on Home Discipleship," *Christianity Today*, February 20, 2020, https://www .christianitytoday.com/2020/02/discipleship-parenting-kids-stay-christian -home-catechesis/.

10. Our church recommends *My First Catechism*, a rendition of the Westminster Shorter Catechism for pre-K to third grade. Starr Meade's family devotionals *Training Hearts, Teaching Minds: Family Devotions Based on the Shorter Catechism* (P&R Publishing, 2000) and *Comforting Hearts, Teaching Minds: Family Devotions Based on the Heidelberg Catechism* (P&R Publishing, 2013), based on the historic confessions of the Reformed church, are also commendable. Terry Johnson's *The Family Worship Book: A Resource Book for Family Devotions* (Christian Focus, 2009) is another classic.

Chapter 4 Incorporation, Not Accommodation

1. Adamczyk and Smith, *Handing Down the Faith*, 110.

2. Another recent study that makes this case is summarized by Stefani McDade in "Taking Kids to Church Matters More Than the 'Right' School, Study Suggests," *Christianity Today*, January 25, 2022, https:// www.christianitytoday.com/2022/01/education-schooling private public -church-attendance-study/.

3. The best overviews on children in worship are Daniel Hyde's *The Nursery of the Holy Spirit: Welcoming Children in Worship* (Wipf and Stock, 2014) and Jason Heleopolous's *Let the Children Worship* (Christian Focus, 2016). They provide more extensive arguments, though it is still worth giving an outline of the biblical argumentation here.

4. Patrick D. Miller, *Deuteronomy* (Cambridge University Press, 1990), 10.

5. In English this concludes at Deuteronomy 29:2.

6. While Deuteronomy was originally written in Hebrew, its Greek translation (LXX) in use in Jesus's day uses the verb *eklesiasas* for the term "assemble." *Eklesiasas* is the verb form of the same term used in the New Testament for church, *eklesia*, the assembly or congregating of the people. The New Testament is intentionally using the vocabulary its original readers would have known. In other words, the congregating of Israel in Deuteronomy 31 is equivalent to the New Testament congregating of the church.

7. The reference to baptism, the promise being to children and to those who are far off, and the connection to the Old Testament covenant context of Deuteronomy 29 are some of the reasons that Presbyterians argue for the baptism of infants.

8. Another question that sometimes arises is what churches should do for kids with ADHD or mental disabilities. In the case of ADHD, there is nothing about the disorder that makes a child less capable of being in a worship service than in a classroom. If a disorder or disability is so severe that a child cannot be in a worship service, they require not an age-focused class but specialized care. Yet the general principles herein still apply: God loves all his children, all his people should be welcome to meet with him in worship, and the church should be hospitable and patient with all present. A good practical guide is Katie Wetherbee and Jolene Philo's *Every Child Welcome: A Ministry Handbook for Including Kids with Special Needs* (Kregel, 2015).

9. Pawel Bartosik outlines a good understanding of this in "Children as a Part of the Church," Theopolis Institute, September 12, 2023, https://theopolisinstitute.com/children-as-a-part-of-the-church/.

10. I'm indebted to my friend Bryan Rhodes, pastor of Grace Presbyterian Church in Alexandria, Louisiana, for this idea, and to Melynda Boyle at Langhorne Presbyterian for putting it together.

11. Ace Collins, *Stories Behind the Great Traditions of Christmas: Discovering the History of Our Favorite Christmas Celebrations* (Zondervan, 2003), 41–46.

12. Teach Us to Worship, accessed July 21, 2025, https://teachustoworship.org/.

Chapter 5 More Than Programs

1. Adamczyk and Smith, *Handing Down the Faith*, 73.

2. Jean M. Twenge, *Generations: The Real Differences Between Gen Z, Millennials, Gen X, Boomers, and Silents—and What They Mean for America's Future* (Atria, 2023), 340–42, 393, 408–11, 443–46.

3. Matthew D. Lieberman, *Social: Why Our Brains Are Wired to Connect* (Crown, 2013), 247.

4. Richard M. Weaver, *Visions of Order: The Cultural Crisis of Our Time* (Intercollegiate Studies Institute, 1995), 113.

5. Adamczyk and Smith, *Handing Down the Faith*, 73–79.

6. Adamczyk and Smith, *Handing Down the Faith*, 73–74.

7. Jonathan Tjarks, "Does My Son Know You?," The Ringer, March 3, 2022, https://www.theringer.com/2022/03/03/health/fatherhood-cancer-jonathan-tjarks.

8. Tjarks, "Does My Son Know You?"

9. Sinclair B. Ferguson's *Children of the Living God* (Banner of Truth, 1987) is one of the most accessible summaries of this.

10. This was my introduction to John Piper. I still remember his sermon series on Romans from this study! The memories of kids are long.

11. Adamczyk and Smith, *Handing Down the Faith*, 209–11; Smith, "Keeping the Faith."

12. Anthony Bradley, "American Evangelicalism Isn't Patriarchal or Feminized. It's Matrilineal," *Mere Orthodoxy*, August 26, 2020, https://mereorthodoxy.com/evangelicals-matrilineal. Making such a sweeping claim is dangerous and risks tuning people out, but Bradley's article on the subject helps make sense of much of the gender-parent dynamic in churches, and the overview provided should at least be given a fair hearing.

13. Bradley, "American Evangelicalism."

Chapter 6 Keeping the Horse Before the Cart

1. Charlotte M. Mason, *Parents and Children* (Living Book Press, 2017), 92–95.

2. That's not to say that large churches are bad or are doing this on purpose, or that large churches or parents seeking churches with kids' ministries don't care about doctrine or substance, but that size is often conflated with vibrancy and vibrancy with quality, and this becomes a tiebreaker.

3. Mimi L. Larson and Robert J. Keeley's *Bridging Theory and Practice in Children's Spirituality: New Directions for Education, Ministry, and Discipleship* (Zondervan, 2020) gives a good overview of the shifting and embedded perspectives on children's ministry.

4. Adamczyk and Smith, *Handing Down the Faith*, 213–16.

5. Kevin DeYoung's *The (Not-So-Secret) Secret to Reaching the Next Generation* (Crossway, 2024), Brian H. Cosby's *Giving Up Gimmicks: Reclaiming Youth Ministry from an Entertainment Culture* (P&R

Publishing, 2012), and Matt Markins's *The Faith of Our Children: Eight Timely Research Insights for Discipling the Next Generation* (Randall House, 2023) provide good, concrete guidance for age-appropriate, high biblical expectations for children's ministries.

6. Smith, "Keeping the Faith."

7. A common complaint of youth group workers is that parents treat youth groups as replacements for discipling their kids. Adamczyk and Smith found that most parents did not view their relationship to youth groups this way (*Handing Down the Faith*, 69). Unfortunately, the model typically embraced by youth workers still functions as a replacement for or ineffective partner to parental influence rather than as a reinforcement of it.

8. Churches should do their due diligence in protecting children and youth who are involved in programs both in the church building and sponsored by the church, and by encouraging prudence that fosters child safety for families in how churches promote interactions between children and other adults. There are many good resources for congregations, and the Safe Church Ministry of the Christian Reformed Church is a commendable model.

9. Cameron Cole, "Why Youth Group Involvement Is Down (and What to Do About It)," The Gospel Coalition, September 6, 2023, https://www .thegospelcoalition.org/article/kids-youth-ministry/.

10. Thomas E. Bergler's *The Juvenilization of American Christianity* (Eerdmans, 2012) and *From Here to Maturity: Overcoming the Juvenilization of American Christianity* (Eerdmans, 2014) are helpful guides on this subject.

11. Sinclair B. Ferguson's *Maturity: Growing Up and Going On in the Christian Life* (Banner of Truth, 2019) provides a good blueprint for this in the life of the church.

12. Since channeling is not about recruiting parents but about parents using resources to reinforce their influence, the godly examples for parents do not have to be parents themselves. Godly, mature adults who never had kids can still serve as examples of wisdom, patience, humility, and biblical teaching.

Chapter 7 Holding On

1. Joshua D. Chatraw and Jack Carson's *Surprised by Doubt: How Disillusionment Can Invite Us into a Deeper Faith* (Brazos Press, 2023) is a good guide to deconstructing and staying within the faith.

2. "Church Dropouts."

3. "Church Dropouts"; Davis, Graham, and Burge, *The Great Dechurching*, 93–95.

4. Adamczyk and Smith, *Handing Down the Faith*, 168–89.

5. Davis, Graham, and Burge, *The Great Dechurching*, 24, 27.

6. Kathleen Nielson's Prayers of a Parent series (P&R Publishing), a beautiful four-volume collection of prayers for parents for their children from infancy through adulthood, is a great resource.

CAMERON SCOTT SHAFFER (PhD candidate, Vrije Universiteit Amsterdam) is the senior pastor of Langhorne Presbyterian Church in Langhorne, Pennsylvania, and serves on the board of directors for the World Reformed Fellowship. He has written for a number of online magazines and journals, including *Reformation21* and *Mere Orthodoxy*.

Connect with Cameron:
CameronShaffer.com